Studying

Human Societies

A Primer and Guide

PATRICK NOLAN

University of South Carolina at Columbia

A Student Supplement for *Human Societies*

ELEVENTH EDITION

PATRICK NOLAN AND GERHARD LENSKI

Paradigm Publishers

Boulder • London

♻ Paradigm Publishers is committed to preserving our environment. This book was printed on recycled paper with 30% post-consumer waste content, saving trees and avoiding the creation of hundreds of gallons of wastewater, tens of pounds of solid waste, more than a hundred pounds of greenhouse gases, and using hundreds fewer kilowatt hours of electricity than if it had been printed on paper manufactured from all virgin fibers.

Copyright © 2004, 2006, 2009 by Paradigm Publishers

Published in the United States by Paradigm Publishers, 3360 Mitchell Lane Suite E, Boulder, Colorado 80301 USA.

Paradigm Publishers is the trade name of Birkenkamp & Company, LLC, Dean Birkenkamp, President and Publisher.

ISBN: 978-1-59451-669-6

Printed and bound in the United States of America on acid free paper that meets the standards of the American National Standard for Permanence of Paper for Printed Library Materials.

11 10 09   1 2 3

Contents

Preface

Although I claim no paranormal powers, and am suspicious of those who do, I am confident that after you have read *Human Societies* you will have a much better understanding of the variety of societies in which humans have lived, why your own society is the way it is, and what it might be like in the future. I also think you will better understand the forces behind world events, such as the rise in terrorism, the large number of "shooting wars" being waged as I write, and the droughts, famines, and political unrest that continually assault societies in sub-Saharan Africa—in short, you will have a better understanding of our world.

It is only fair to warn you, however, that *Human Societies* is very different from other introductory sociology texts. It tries to develop a general understanding of what makes societies the way they are by comparing them to one another in a systematic way. To promote a better understanding of industrial societies, such as our own, it compares them to very different kinds of societies in very different situations. This means that you will spend a good deal of time studying societies very different from your own, and the view the book will take of industrial societies will probably be unfamiliar to you. Thus, you will *not* be able to rely very much on your own *personal experiences*.

Since most of you have not lived in a hunting-gathering band, or a horticultural or agricultural village, or even an *early* industrial or industrializing society, your experiences will not tell you very much about how they are organized, or what life in such societies is like. To a certain extent, then, "common sense" is going to be an obstacle rather than an aid in this course. You are often going to think that you *already know* answers to questions when you really don't.

For instance, the "answers" that readily come to mind concerning such important questions as:

- Can social inequality be eliminated?
- Is war an unavoidable consequence of human nature?
- Why do men and women perform different roles in society?
- Are individuals smarter today than they were 10,000 or 20,000 years ago?

are not necessarily consistent with the evidence that archaeologists, anthropologists, and sociologists have amassed on these issues. Every society provides its members with *cultural* explanations of why things are the way they are, but it is the role of social science to *test* these explanations against the best available evidence and to distinguish what is "myth" from what is fact. As I will try to show in the first chapter of this primer and guide, if the best available evidence is *consistent* with an explanation, that does not guarantee that it is true, but if the evidence is *inconsistent* with an explanation, then there is good reason to be skeptical.

I promise you that the textbook and the information it presents about human societies will challenge you to think in new ways. For instance, although in our personal lives we are used to thinking in terms of months, years, or decades, in order to understand the major trends and developments in human societies, the text will challenge you to think in terms of *centuries,* and in some cases *thousands* of years.

Ironically, when viewed in such a time frame, a number of things that our cultural beliefs imply are aspects of a basic and unchanging "human nature" turn out instead to be relatively new and recent responses to the advanced technology and enlarged scale of modern societies, and some things that our cultural beliefs imply are recent developments appear to have been present in societies since our species first appeared on this planet.

I say this not to worry or intimidate you, but to help prepare you for this text and the course it is used in. The key point to remember is that, since you cannot rely on your own personal experience, you will have to *learn* the material presented in the text and in class. You will have to approach this course the same way you would any other course that covers material that you are unfamiliar with (e.g., history, physics, literature, astronomy). You cannot rely on "common sense" and your experiences as useful guides.

Although the knowledge you have gained from personal experience may not prepare you for much of what this course will cover, things you may have learned in *other courses*—anthropology, history, political science, economics, and even biology—may well enhance your understanding of what is covered in it. Similarly, what you learn in this course should help you to integrate and make sense of a number of things you have learned or will encounter in other courses.

This primer and guide to *Human Societies* is intended to help you to get the maximum benefit from the course, and to help you to achieve the best possible grade. The advice it offers is based on my own experience working with several thousand students, using this text for more than thirty years, and in helping to write this and the last four editions of *Human Societies.*

In the introduction that follows, I will provide a strategy for reading *Human Societies,* as well as tips on reading tables, taking notes, and taking exams. The ensuing chapters contain summaries and discussions of each of the chapters, lists of important terms, quizzes and study questions that allow you to test your knowledge and prepare for exams, and suggestions for further reading on the topics covered.

I hope this primer and guide makes *Human Societies,* and the course you are using it in, a more enjoyable and rewarding experience for you. Please let me know if you found it useful, or if you have suggestions on how it might be improved, by e-mail at pnolan@sc.edu or at the mailing address below.

Best wishes,

Patrick Nolan
Department of Sociology
University of South Carolina
Columbia, SC 29208

Introduction

General Tips, Guidelines, and Strategies

I. HOW TO READ THE TEXT

A. Fundamentals

You may think it odd that there is a section of *Studying Human Societies* giving advice about how to read the text. After all, you've done a great deal of reading before you entered college. Nonetheless, I have found over the years that one of the most serious barriers to doing well in the introductory course is not knowing *how* to read the text.

The primary cause of difficulty is trying to read the text the same casual way you can read less demanding and less detailed things. Trust me, it doesn't work. *Human Societies* is written for college-level students. It has not been watered down, and it does not assume you are stupid or insult your intelligence. Since it is a *college* textbook, however, you should not expect to be able to read it the same way you would a novel, newspaper, or magazine.

In fact, you should expect to have to read the chapters MORE THAN ONCE in order to understand them fully. You will also find that you will have problems following the text if you try to read it at the same time that you are watching TV or trying to carry on a conversation with friends.

In addition, you should expect to encounter words that you have not seen or heard before. Although there is a glossary defining key sociological terms pages 351 to 358 in *Human Societies*—you should have a good college dictionary handy when you are reading.[1]

Looking up words may seem a tedious and thankless task, but it is an effective way to expand your vocabulary.[2] Furthermore, since many people judge a person's intelligence by his or her vocabulary, reading this text and looking up the meanings of unfamiliar words will not only help you attain a good grade in the course, but may also increase the respect of friends, colleagues, and prospective employers.

B. First Reading

The first thing you should do is look over the course outline or syllabus provided by your instructor. See when you are scheduled to discuss or be examined on different materials. Look at the schedule of your other courses and try to find a time that you can routinely devote to assigned reading. *Schedule* your reading the same way you would any other important activity (such as sleeping, eating, and exercising). Turn off the TV and radio. If you have noisy roommates, find a quiet place on campus or in the library that is free of distractions.

Although you should plan to read each chapter more than once, you will not read the chapter the same way each time. First, you should read the material once BEFORE it is scheduled for class discussion. This will help you to better understand the class discussion or lecture. It will also prepare you for possible "pop" quizzes," and you will be able to participate in class discussions.

Just before you actually begin to read the chapter for the first time, open the book to the assigned chapter and simply page through it from beginning to end. Read the headings and subheadings. These constitute the outline of the chapter. The main headings are the main points or topics, and the subheadings are the details or examples of those topics. Try to get an overall sense of what the chapter covers. Look at the pictures; read the captions.[3]

You may find that this raises questions in your mind. That's good. In fact, you may want to write these questions down. When you read something to find an answer to a question, it will make more sense, and you will remember more of it afterwards. If your first reading of the chapter doesn't answer your questions, ask your professor or teaching assistant in class. Class meetings provide an *opportunity* for you to get answers to your questions. You shouldn't think that your questions are a problem or a distraction. Unless you are explicitly told otherwise, questions are generally *welcomed*.

If the question requires a lengthy answer and time is short, or if it might take the scheduled discussion too far afield, your professor or graduate teaching assistant[4] may suggest that you discuss it after class or during office hours. This does not mean that they are putting you down or think your question is without value. Take it as an honest invitation. Follow up on it; it's YOUR class, YOUR education.

C. Second Reading

After lecture and class discussion, you should READ THE CHAPTER AGAIN. This time read it *closely*. You will find that it makes more sense now, and you should not expect to have difficulty with any part of it. If you do, WRITE YOUR QUESTIONS OR PROBLEMS DOWN. Talk to your professor or graduate teaching assistant about them during their office hours. If their scheduled office hours are not convenient for you, try to make an appointment for a better time. But don't ignore any problems with the chapter after the second reading. They probably won't go away, and may well get worse, especially if this lack of understanding interferes with your ability to understand material in later chapters.

II. HOW TO READ TABLES

The ability to read data displayed in tables is an essential and important skill. Much of the information in this text, and in texts for other social science classes, is presented in percentage tables. Most employers today expect employees to be able to evaluate information in tables, and as citizens and consumers we are continually confronted with tables, graphs, and charts that we must be able to read and understand if we are to make informed and intelligent decisions. Thus the ability to read tables is not simply a skill needed to succeed in college courses; it is essential for success in the world of work and for active and effective citizenship.

As with most other skills, time and effort are needed to become *expert* at reading and analyzing tables. Nonetheless, a few simple rules and exercises can take much of the mystery out of table-reading and will enable you to better understand the tables in this book.

A. Fundamentals

The most important thing you need to understand in order to read tables is the *logic* of the percentage table. Tables are used to show whether or not *one thing makes a difference for something else,* and they do so in a clear and relatively unambiguous way. Unlike prose or talk, which is often vague and inexact in describing the impact of one thing on another, tables make direct comparisons between specific numbers. This allows you to see not only whether one thing affects another, but also *how much* of an effect it has.

To see if something makes a difference for something else, you need to compare *conditional distributions.* Conditional distributions reveal how one thing varies or changes depending on the value, or condition, of something else. Let's consider an example to see what this means.

Suppose we want to know if some types of societies are *more likely* to have slavery than other types. To get the information we need to answer this question, we can go to the data assembled by Murdock and his associates (for a general description of the data and where it can be obtained, see *Human Societies,* appendix, pages 362–363).

If you were to consult these data, you would find that 19 of the 166 hunting and gathering societies (for which we have data) have some form of slavery; 22 of the 143 simple horticultural societies have slavery; 187 of the 225 advanced horticultural have slavery; and 41 of the 91 agrarian have slavery.[5] We can examine this more easily if we display the data in columns and rows, and add information on industrial societies:

Type of Society	Number with Slavery	Total Number of Societies
Hunting-Gathering	19	166
Simple Horticultural	22	143
Advanced Horticultural	187	225
Agrarian	41	91
Advanced Industrial	0	16

Examination of these figures suggests that advanced horticultural societies are the most likely to have slavery. More of them (187) have slavery than any other type of society in the table. We can't be sure that this larger number indicates a greater *likelihood* of slavery, however, because there are more advanced horticultural societies in the table (225) than any other type of society. It could be the case that there are more advanced horticultural societies with slavery *simply because there are more advanced horticultural societies in the table.* Recall that our original question was whether or not the *likelihood* of slavery was different in the different types of societies.

It would be much easier to answer this question if there were *exactly the same number of each type of society.* Then the number with slavery could be directly compared. If there were exactly the same number of each type, differences in the number with slavery would indicate differences in the *likelihood* or *probability* of slavery. Moreover, a small difference would indicate a slight difference in likelihood, and a large difference would indicate a major difference in likelihood.

Fortunately there is a way to make this kind of comparison even though we have information for different numbers of each type of society. The way to do it is to convert the *numbers* of societies with slavery into the *percentages* of societies with slavery. As the term *percent* indicates, this is a way of "pretending" there are exactly *one hundred* societies of each type. In other words, when we calculate *percentages* for the table above, we will get the number of societies that would have slavery if there were exactly 100 societies of each type in the table.

Differences in these numbers (percentages) among societal types, therefore, cannot be a result of differences in the number of societies in each category. Percentaging is thus a simple "trick" to make comparisons among societal types more meaningful.

How are percentages calculated? In the table above, we would calculate the percentage of hunting and gathering societies with slavery by taking the *number* of hunting and gathering societies *with slavery,* dividing it by the *total number* of hunting and gathering societies, and multiplying the result (the *proportion* with slavery) by 100. Using the numbers from the example above, and starting with the first row:

19 divided by 166 equals .114
.114 multiplied by 100 equals 11.4 percent
or "rounded" to the nearest whole number, 11 percent.

This number indicates that if there were exactly 100 hunting-gathering societies, 11 of them would have slavery. Repeating this procedure for simple horticulturalists:

22 divided by 143 equals .154
.154 multiplied by 100 equals 15.4 percent
or "rounded" to the nearest whole number, 15 percent.

If there were exactly 100 simple horticultural societies, 15 of them would have slavery. Before you read the rest of this discussion, calculate the other percentages for yourself and enter them in the following table.[6]

Type of Society	Percentage with Slavery
Hunting and Gathering	11
Simple Horticultural	15
Advanced Horticultural	[ ]
Agrarian	[ ]
Advanced Industrial	0

Now that they can be directly compared, some things become very clear. First, advanced horticultural societies *are* the most likely to have slavery. *In fact, almost all of them do.*

It is also apparent that some differences are small, while others are quite large. On the one hand, the difference between hunters-gatherers and simple horticulturalists is quite small. They are very similar—neither is very likely to have slavery. On the other hand, they are both very different from advanced horticultural and agrarian societies.

Moreover, although agrarian societies are more likely than hunting and gathering or simple horticultural societies to have slavery, they are only about half as likely to have slavery as are advanced horticulturalists. Thus even though our first impression based on the *number* of societies with slavery was correct—advanced horticulturalists were the most likely to have slavery—the percentages allow us to make more precise comparisons of the effects of subsistence technology on the likelihood of slavery.

In terms of the earlier discussion, the percentage for each type of society represents the distribution of slavery for *that condition* of subsistence technology.[7] Comparing the conditional distributions shows whether or not "type" of society *makes a difference for the likelihood of slavery.* If it does not, then the percentages for the different types will be very similar to one another. This would indicate that differences in subsistence technology did *not* affect the likelihood of slavery.

This is the case, in fact, for the comparison of hunters-gatherers and simple horticulturalists. The table shows that *this* difference in subsistence technology does not make much of a difference for the likelihood of slavery. Slavery is about equally likely, or to be more precise, equally *un*likely in these types of societies. Hunting and gathering and simple horticultural societies are very similar in regard to the likelihood of slavery. The very large differences found between these societies and agrarian and advanced horticultural, however, indicate that these conditions (subsistence technologies) make *quite a difference* for the likelihood of slavery.

This logic is common to virtually all the comparisons we will make in *Human Societies*. Regardless of whether it is a graph, a bar chart, or a table, we are most interested in comparing *conditional distributions*. Therefore, one of the first steps in reading one of them is to determine what the "conditions" and "conditional distributions" are.

Because in *Human Societies* we are primarily interested in comparing different types of societies, type of society is usually the condition, and the distributions of other traits (such as slavery) by type of society are the conditional distributions.

The percentage tables you encounter in other contexts will not always have societal type as the condition, and the rows will not necessarily constitute the conditional distributions. In such cases, the most straightforward way to determine which are the conditions and which are the conditional distributions is to examine the way the percentages have been computed. This is especially easy if the total percentages are reported in the table. If the percentages in *the rows* total 100 percent, *the rows are the conditional distributions*; if the percentages in *the columns* total 100 percent, *the columns are the conditional distributions*.[8]

Since you are interested in seeing if the *conditions* make a difference, if the columns total 100 percent, compare within the rows (across columns); if the rows total 100 percent, make comparisons within the columns (across rows). Thus, whichever way the percentages total 100 percent, *make comparisons the other way*.[9]

In *Human Societies* the rows of percentage tables are usually the conditional distributions, and we make comparisons across rows (e.g., 11 percent vs. 15 percent in the slavery table above).[10] In the graphs and bar charts, the columns are the conditional distributions, and we make comparisons across columns. For example, the graph on page 71 of *Human Societies* (Figure 4.3) shows that while only 7 percent of advanced horticultural societies have complex status systems, 51 percent of agrarian societies do.

B. Variations

Information is also presented in slightly different ways in the text. Instead of being a *percentage* table (the *title* of the table will tell you if it is a percentage table or some other kind of table), some tables simply present information (dates, numbers, per capita income figures, etc.) for different societies or different types of societies.[11] For example, Table 5.1 (page 81) shows the time period in which important technological innovations were made and the accelerating rate of innovation across time periods, and Table 12.1 (page 264) shows the income of the fifteen richest people in the world.

Table 4.2 (page 70) presents the average (median) size of the different types of societies, and Table 5.3 (page 86) presents the average (median) size of societies with differing degrees of reliance on hunting and gathering.[12] Table 6.1 (page 10) displays the average (median) population density of the different types of societies. Table 7.1 (page 151) shows the average age at death for people living in different periods of the agrarian era.

A few tables and figures *illustrate abstract ideas with hypothetical information*. For instance, Table 3.1 (page 52) shows how the amount of cultural information in a society affects the *potential* for making inventions; Table 3.2 (page 54) illustrates a "paradox" in societal evolution; Table 10.4 (page 227) shows the effects of fixed and variable costs on the development of monopolies in industrial societies.

Most of the tables and figures for industrial societies either show changes in a single country over time (e.g., agricultural productivity in the United States, Table 10.1 on page 216; the percentage of African-Americans in middle-class occupations from 1940 to 2006 in the United States, Figure 12.4 on page 271); a list or set of societies over time (e.g., government spending as a percentage of GDP from 1870 to 2005, Table 10.6 on page 230; proportion of elite positions held by women in selected industrial societies, Table 13.5 on page 291; extension of the franchise in western Europe 1830 to 1975, Figure 11.1 on page 248) or make comparisons among industrial societies (e.g., household income shares, Table 12.2 on page 265).[13]

The tables in Chapter 14 compare contemporary hybrid societies[14]—"industrializing agrarian" and "industrializing horticultural" societies—with one another, and with industrial societies (e.g., levels of political and civil rights, Table 14.3 on page 308; shares of total income, Table 14.5 on page 311), or show trends or rates of change in these types of societies over time (e.g., average rates of economic and population growth, Table 14.2 on page 304).

These and other tables in the text will be discussed in more detail in the corresponding chapters of the text and *Study Guide*.

III. HOW TO TAKE NOTES ON CLASSROOM MATERIALS

Taking useful notes requires the careful balancing of two equally troublesome tendencies. One is the urge to try to write *everything* down. The other is the urge to write *nothing* down.

The first tendency interferes with understanding and is ultimately futile. Unless you are a trained court stenographer, it will be impossible for you to write *everything* down. Furthermore, while you are struggling to do so, you will miss a good deal of what is said. My advice is, don't try.

The second tendency rests on the false assumption that you will remember everything you hear. Trust me, you won't. Even if you have an excellent memory, without class notes to remind you, you will forget much of what was said in the days and weeks that pass before you are examined on the material.[15]

Note-taking is not an exact science, and I can't offer any magical or scientifically proven techniques that will solve all problems. Nonetheless, I can offer some suggestions that may help to improve your note-taking and preparation for exams.

A. In Class

First, bring *Human Societies* to class. If the lecture or discussion is progressing through the chapter, try to page through at the same pace. If you do, you will have definitions, charts, figures, and tables at your fingertips. Then if a definition is cited, you will not have to write it down word-for-word. Instead you can mark the text, make a note of the page number in your notes, and copy the definition later.

In the meantime, you can pay attention to the discussion of it in the lecture or class discussion. You might be tempted not to follow through by writing out definitions and filling in abbreviations in your notes. This is usually a mistake. Writing out something you have seen or heard will reinforce your knowledge of it. You may, in fact, find that you can write out a word-for-word or nearly word-for-word definition of it on an exam if you have actually written it out in your notes after class.

In any event, the important point is not to be distracted from the class by *writing down something that is already spelled out in the text.* The same point applies to the tables and graphs. If you have your text with you, you can follow the discussion of the information rather than getting bogged down writing or copying numbers. It is generally more important to *understand* the table and know *what it says,* than to memorize specific numbers in it.[16]

If your professor puts an outline of the lecture on the board, or indicates at the beginning of the lecture the main points that will be covered, copy them in the margin or at the top of your notebook. This is the skeleton, or organization, of the lecture. The lecture will fill in the details, give examples, and explain these points.

If you have the outline, filling in the blanks will be relatively easy. If you don't, you will have to make judgments based on the emphasis and time given the point by your professor or graduate teaching assistant. Often they will say things such as "this is important" or "there are three points you should remember about.   .   ."   These are likely to be important *headings* that are followed by specific examples and details. Sometimes your professor will put them on the board before discussion of them. Copy them in the margin of your notes. Then put them individually into the body of your notes and fill in the details below as they are presented in class.

If they're not on the board and you miss one, or if your professor says s/he is going to discuss *four* key points and then discusses only *three,* raise your hand and ask about the missing one. Your professor and your classmates will generally welcome such a clarification.

You may also want to scribble the names of references (books, journal articles, and the like) mentioned in the lecture in the margins of your notes. This may prove helpful if you want more information on the topic for yourself or for a term paper or class project. In any event, if you write it down, it won't take much time or space to record it, and you'll have it if you need it later.

B. After Class

As soon as you are able after class—immediately after class if you can; that morning, afternoon, or evening if you can't—rewrite or recopy your notes. This is the time to try to add details, to fill in definitions and figures. The sooner you do this, the more you will remember, and the more you will be able to fill in. If there are points that are unclear, you can make a note to yourself to ask about it in the next class (rather than discovering this *the night before an exam* when it is too late to do anything about it).

But perhaps even more important, the sooner you return to and recopy your notes, the more class material you will retain. Memory fades with time, but if you review what you have learned shortly afterwards, you will remember more of it longer. Thus, even though you should expect to forget *some* of the material before the exam, you will remember much more of it than you would have if you hadn't returned to, and reviewed, your notes. *If you did nothing else, this alone would probably significantly raise your grade in the course.*

If, in addition to this, you also study just prior to the exam, you will find that since you *already* remember more, you have less to (re)learn and can therefore spend your time studying more effectively and efficiently. This is especially important if you have other courses and activities that are putting demands on your time and effort.

Therefore, what might seem at first to be a more time-consuming and inefficient method of study is actually *more efficient.* Applying these methods should not only raise

6. According to *Cows, Pigs, Wars, and Witches,* the most important contribution that cows make to the Indian economy is dung.

The correct answers are: 1. d, 2. b, 3. a, 4. d, 5. t, 6. f.[18]

Be sure you know *why* the answers you selected are correct or incorrect. If you're not sure, read the question again and review the discussion above. If you're still not sure, ask your professor or graduate teaching assistant to help you with them.

You may occasionally encounter a word that you don't understand on a test. If you do, ask about it. It may be a misspelling, which can be corrected, or your professor or graduate teaching assistant may be able to tell you what it means. On the other hand, it may be something you should have learned but didn't. My best advice is to ask. The worst that can happen is that they won't be able to help you. The best is that it may help you to get a question correct that you otherwise would have misunderstood and missed.

Also remember my warning in the preface about "common sense." Base your answers on *what you have learned in the readings and lectures,* not on what you "knew" before enrolling in the course. As I noted in the preface, "common sense" often leads us to believe that human societies are simply reflections of "human nature." This may lead you to think that social organization and behavior are pretty much the same in all societies. They aren't. It may also lead you to think that "instincts" explain human behavior. They don't. You might also think that societies like ours can send people to the bottom of the oceans and to the moon and back because we are more intelligent than people were thousands of years ago. We aren't. There is no evidence that we are more intelligent than people were 20,000 years ago!

I can't go through *all* the cases where "common sense" might steer you wrong without reproducing most of the text and lectures for the course, but these examples should serve as a warning. Don't think that "common sense" and your personal experiences are going to be much help in taking tests. If anything, they are likely to be *problems.* Often they will make an incorrect answer seem right, or lead you to believe you already have the answers to questions before you have mastered the information in the text and in your notes.

B. Essay Questions

The most important piece of advice I can offer for answering an essay question is to read the question *carefully* and be sure you *answer the question that is asked.* Grading policies vary by professor, but an *excellent* answer to a question *not asked* will *not* be graded *excellent.* In general, the more directly the answer addresses the question asked, the better the grade.[19]

The next best advice is to *organize* your answer. As you think about the question, a number of things will come to mind. Start to list them in the margins of your answer book, or on your question sheet. Just *list* them at first, don't try to fill in details or write out the answer.

After you have listed all the things you think are involved in the answer to the question, take a moment and reflect upon their relative importance. Then start to organize the list into the outline of an answer to the question. As I indicated, you can scribble this in the margins or on the question sheet. Don't worry about crossing things out or drawing arrows to move things around in the outline—this is only a device to *organize your thinking.* Once you've completed your answer, you can cross it out or erase it. Like a scaffold, when its purpose has been fulfilled, it can be discarded.

After you've completed this outline, use it to organize your answer. It will help make your answer more coherent, and will keep you from forgetting things you want to mention.

If the question asks you to draw a conclusion or make a judgment and then document or present evidence to support it, state your conclusion or judgment clearly and bluntly *right at the start* of the answer. Follow this with the evidence that you base it on or feel supports your answer. Present this evidence in a coherent manner, indicating the relative *importance* of each item. Indicate what your *most important* reasons are, or what the *strongest* evidence is in favor of it. This will help keep the details or specifics from obscuring or getting in the way of the main points of your answer.

C. "Pop" Quizzes

The authors of *Human Societies* have strongly recommended that your professor use "pop" quizzes in this course. This is because "pop" quizzes (a) provide an *incentive* and *reward* for keeping up with the reading on a regular basis (i.e., a high "pop" quiz average will raise your grade),[20] and (b) provide a basis and a focus for class discussion.

As these objectives indicate, "pop" quizzes are not designed to be "tricky" or to test in-depth knowledge of a topic. The best "pop" quiz questions are those that are *easy* to get right if you have read the assignment, and virtually *impossible* to get right if you haven't. As I indicated earlier, if you read through the material before class, the "pop" quizzes should not be a problem for you. If there is some part of the reading that you had difficulty with and you are worried that it might be the subject of a "pop" quiz question, take the offensive. Ask about it at the beginning of class. As I noted earlier, questions are generally *welcomed,* and you will be achieving the second objective of "pop" quizzes by asking the question.

D. Study Guide Help

The *Study Guide* will provide quiz questions at the end of each chapter that will help you to prepare for the exams and "pop" quizzes. They will provide experience with answering questions, and should help you decide if you have prepared sufficiently and have an adequate grasp of the material. After you have read the chapter for a second time, take the test in the *Study Guide. To get the maximum benefit, it is important to replicate actual test conditions as closely as possible.*[21] Sit down and answer *all* the questions to the best of your ability *without* paging back through the *Study Guide,* your lecture notes, or *Human Societies.* This is the only way to accurately assess how well you have mastered the material. Used in any other way, the quizzes will not help very much and may actually *lower* your performance by giving you a false sense of confidence.

To score your exam, divide the number *you had correct* by the *total number of questions* and multiply by 100. In general, a score of 90–100 is excellent, 80–89 is good, 70–79 is fair, 60–69 is poor, and below 60 is failing.

After you grade your exam, be sure you know *why* your answers were right or wrong. If you can't figure out why an answer is right or wrong, ask your teaching assistant or professor. If they can't help, you can reach me by snail-mail at: Department of Sociology, University of South Carolina, Columbia, SC 29208, or by E-mail at: pnolan@sc.edu.[22]

V. KEY POINTS IN REVIEW

    A. *Reading the Text*
        Read each assignment TWICE:
            a. First skim it before class to get an overview.
            b. Then read it again after class for details.
    B. *Reading Tables*
        Percentaging equalizes the number of societies.
        Conditional distributions reveal the effects of conditions on something else.
    C. *Taking Notes on Class Materials*
        Bring your book to class.
        Don't try to write *everything* down.
        Rewrite your notes after class.
    D. *Taking Tests*
        Read each question *carefully*.
        Answer the question asked.
        Don't trust "common sense."
        Use an outline to organize answers to essay questions.
    E. *General*
        When you have a question, ask it!

RECOMMENDED READING"

1. *Say It with Figures,* by Hans Zeisel (New York: Harper & Row, 1985). A very readable source of information on preparing and reading percentage tables.

2. *The Sociological Method,* by Stephen Cole (Chicago: Rand McNally, 1976). Explains and provides examples of how percentage tables can be used to test sociological theories.

3. *Cows, Pigs, Wars, and Witches: The Riddles of Culture,* by Marvin Harris (NY: Random House, 1974). Down-to-earth explanations of puzzling cultural beliefs by an eminent anthropologist.

EXERCISES AND QUESTIONS

To test your knowledge of percentage tables, calculate the percentages for the following data and answer the questions that follow.

    According to Murdock's *Ethnographic Atlas,*[24] belief in a "creator-God who is concerned with the moral conduct of humans" is found in 4 of 100 hunting and gathering societies, 10 of 102 simple horticultural societies, 27 of 176 advanced horticultural societies, and 56 of 88 agrarian societies. Calculate the percentage of each of the types of societies that have such belief and enter them in the table below. Then answer the questions that follow the table.

Type of Society	Percentage with the Belief in a "Creator-God"
Hunting and Gathering	
Simple Horticultural	
Advanced Horticultural	
Agrarian	

1. Which type of society is *least* likely to have such a belief?

2. Which type of society is *most* likely to have such a belief?

3. What percentage of advanced horticultural societies do NOT have such a belief?

(You can check your calculations by comparing your percentages to those in Figure 4.4 on page 72 of *Human Societies*.)

NOTES

[1] If you come across a word you do not know and you are without a dictionary, write the word down and look it up as soon as you are able.

[2] You may think it is odd for a person with an extensive vocabulary to consult a dictionary, but it is exactly that kind of dictionary usage that develops an extensive vocabulary! You would not be surprised that someone with big muscles lifts weights.

[3] Chapter summaries in this *Primer and Guide* will help at this stage of the reading and in reviewing for exams, but you should not rely on them as *substitutes* for reading the chapters in the text.

[4] If you are taking this course in a large lecture hall, there is a good chance that your professor is assisted by one or more graduate students. They are studying to be sociologists and are assisting in your class to gain valuable teaching experience by working with a seasoned professor.

[5] Types of societies are distinguished by the way they get or produce the necessities of life *(subsistence technology)*. Very simply, those that forage for what they need are hunters-gatherers; those that grow their food in gardens are horticulturalists (advanced horticulturalists use *metal* tools, while simple horticulturalists do not); those that farm with plows are agriculturalists; and those that use machines to make and get what they need are industrial societies. The method of classifying and the reasons for this classification are discussed in more detail in Chapter 4 and in the appendix of *Human Societies*. These types of societies are further described and compared in Chapters 5–13 of *Human Societies*.

[6] To check your answers, compare them with the numbers in the top line of Figure 6.5, p. 126 in *Human Societies*.

[7] The other half of the conditional distribution, societies *without* slavery, is not shown in the table. This is because it is a perfect mirror-image of societies *with* slavery. Subtracting the percentage *with* slavery from 100 would yield the percentage *without* slavery.

[8] The percentages may not always total exactly 100 percent—sometimes they might be slightly more than 100 percent, other times slightly less. This is because of the "rounding" done to simplify the numbers presented in tables.

[9] Put another way: if the totals are at the right, compare up and down; if the totals are at the bottom, compare right to left.

[10] "E.g." is an abbreviation for the Latin *exempli gratia,* which means "for instance." It is used to give *examples* of what is being discussed. Another commonly used abbreviation is "i.e." It stands for the Latin *id est,* which means "that is." It is used to *define* what is being discussed.

[11] *Per capita* is Latin for "per head." Per capita figures tell how much of something there is per *person* in a community or society. To calculate a per capita figure, the total amount of something is *divided* by the total population. In some cases this will produce a very small number (for example, .002). When it does, the per capita figure is sometimes *multiplied* by 1,000 or 100,000 to get a figure per *1,000 persons* or per *100,000 persons* (the *.002* per capita figure would be *2* per 1,000 persons, or *200* per 100,000 persons).

[12] The median is the number in the middle of a series of numbers arranged in order of size—half the cases are larger and half are smaller than the median (see the boxed insert, "Science and Measurement," on page 69 of *Human Societies*).

[13] Tables 11.2 and 11.3 (pages 256–257) provide information on the relationship between occupational class and political party preference. Because these tables require a more technical discussion of percentage tables, I will postpone discussion of them until Chapter 11 of the *Study Guide.*

[14] A "hybrid" society is one that relies on an admixture of two very different technologies for subsistence.

[15] I have read research reports that indicated that many people who think their memories are deteriorating, because they are having problems remembering things, often have excellent memories. The problem is that since they have excellent memories, they are trying to rely on them *too much.* They expect to remember *everything,* and that is an unrealistic expectation.

[16] With modern word-processing technology, some of these tables may even appear in your exams.

[17] This is why they are sometimes referred to as "objective" questions. There is an "objectively" true answer. In contrast, some people consider essay questions to be more "subjective" in the sense that opinion and judgment enter more directly into the answer and its evaluation.

[18] Notice that what makes these questions "objective" is the fact that they all ask *what Harris says.* Thus even though there might be disagreement among experts about the issues being discussed, what *Harris says* can be determined objectively.

[19] On the other hand, I cannot, in good conscience, tell you to leave a question you are required to answer *blank* if you don't have a direct answer to the question asked. If the choice is between answering a *different* question and leaving it blank, answer a different question. It will at least allow you to demonstrate that you have learned something. You might even include an honest explanation of why you are doing so. Professors' policies vary—some will grade an answer to a different question the same as a blank (0); others may give some points—I will generally give it a *failing grade* (less than 60 percent) but not a 0. *Keep the answer short, however, or go back to it later, to be sure that you have sufficient time to answer the other questions on the exam.*

[20] "I.e." is the abbreviation for the Latin *id est* discussed in footnote 10 above.

[21] If the answers are already marked in your study guide, have someone erase the answers or recopy the questions. If you simply scan already-answered questions, you will have no idea how many you would have answered correctly on your own. This is especially true for the fill-in-the-blank questions.

[22] You can also send comments about the *Study Guide* or suggestions for how it might be improved to me at these addresses.

[23] Remember that if your bookstore does not have, or if you don't want to buy, recommended books but you do want to consult them, *you can probably find them in your college library.*

[24] More information on this important data set can be found on pages 68–69 and pages 362–363 of *Human Societies*.

1

The Human Condition

CHAPTER SUMMARY

Macrosociology is defined as the comparative (scientific) study of human societies. Society is defined, its role as an adaptive mechanism for many species is discussed, and signals and symbols are distinguished. Similarities and differences between humans and other primates are identified, and the importance of society and symbolic culture for human survival is discussed. The chapter ends with a discussion of modeling and the basic model of ecological-evolutionary theory, EET (Figure 1.2), which will be explored and elaborated in the following chapters. It is followed by an excursus that presents a brief history of sociology and its relation to other social sciences.

Our species, *Homo sapiens sapiens,* has been on this planet for at least 100,000 years. Chapter 1 uses the image of a family photo album to dramatize the most important features of our experience in this period. First, it shows how *slow* social change was for most of this period. This is something that is hard for us to appreciate, since we live in a society where fundamental change is so common and rapid. Second, it shows how *recent* key historical events have been when viewed in the context of this time frame, and how social change has accelerated in recent millennia.[1]

Sociology is defined on page 4 as: "A branch of modern science . . . [that] . . . has made the study of human societies its chief concern." Two things in this definition are worth emphasizing. First, *science.* Sociology attempts to develop knowledge about societies and the forces affecting them by employing *scientific* methods. Your professor may go into more detail about these methods in class, but there are a few key aspects of these methods that you need to be aware of.

Scientific knowledge is cumulative and is based on systematic comparisons. It is *tested* with empirical[2] evidence. Because it is repeatedly tested, scientific knowledge is subject to revision and change based on future evidence. *Falsifiability* means that the theory or hypothesis must *pass* a test that it is possible to fail. Only theories and hypotheses that *survive* repeated tests are retained.[3] Those that repeatedly fail are modified and retested, or they are rejected.[4]

The second point in the definition worth emphasizing is that it is the science of *human* societies. Social organization is not unique to human beings. A variety of other species of animals live in societies (e.g., see photos on pages 7 and 8 of *Human Societies*). That is not to say that the forms of social organization are the same—they aren't—but it does mean that living in societies does not distinguish humans from other animals. In fact, there is overwhelming evidence that humans *inherited* social organization from their prehuman ancestors.

Social organization appears to have evolved in a number of animal lines because it increases the chances of survival—it is a means of *adaptation,* a way of adjusting to and coping with the environment.

The most essential adaptive feature of social organization is *cooperation*. Animals who live in societies can do things collectively that they are unable to do as isolated individuals. *Human* societies are defined on page 8. In addition to the presence of a broad range of cooperative activities, to be a society a human population must also be politically *autonomous* or self-directing. This added requirement ensures that subgroups (e.g., families, communities) of larger social systems (e.g., villages, states) are not mistaken for societies.

The environments that human societies have adapted to can be broken into two dimensions. There are first the biological and physical features of the environment—plants (flora) and animals (fauna); climate, rainfall, terrain—referred to as the *biophysical* environment. In addition, there are the surrounding human societies, which constitute the *social* environment.

To cope with these environments, human societies have accumulated diverse bodies of useful **information**. These bodies of information include the *genetic* information that has been passed on to humans through millions of years of *biological* evolution. Some key elements of this genetic information are those that have given us the ability to *learn* so much, and the related ability to develop and to communicate with **symbols**.[5]

All social animals have to be able to communicate in some way. Without *communication* they would not be able to "cooperate." Nonetheless, only humans have demonstrated the ability to *create* symbols and symbol systems. Other social animals communicate primarily by means of **signals**.

The key difference between **signals** and **symbols** is that the form and "meaning" of a **signal** are *genetically* determined, whereas the form and meaning of a **symbol** are *socially* determined. Animals that communicate with signals are essentially *born* with the ability both to make and to respond to the signals of their species. The advantage to this kind of communication is that it doesn't have to be learned, and signals don't have to be interpreted. The weakness is that there is a limit to the number and kinds of things that can be communicated.

In contrast, the connection between a symbol and its meaning is socially determined (e.g., see the boxed insert "Fifteen Ways to Say 'I Love You'" on page 14 of *Human Societies*). The strength of this form of communication is its flexibility. Even simple symbol systems like Morse code (dots and dashes) or computer language ('+' and '–' or '0' and '1') can encode any number of messages—all of Shakespeare, the Bible, etc. In fact, there is *no limit* to the information that can be encoded and transmitted by symbols.[6] As we will see in the next chapter, the ability to create symbols makes it possible for humans to create **symbolic culture**. And although social organization may not be unique to human beings, *symbolic culture* is.

Thus human societies are greatly influenced by the information coded in our genes, and by the information coded in our symbolic cultures.

Sociologists have found **models** to be a very effective way to convey abstract information about the patterns of relationships or connections between things. Consider the model presented in Figure 1.2 on page 18. The arrows represent "flows" of influence or effects. Think of them as "pipes" through which water is flowing. The water flows in the directions of the arrows from box to box.

At the center of the figure is a box representing the social and cultural characteristics of a society (e.g., its size, the nature of its political system, its economy). Arrows, indicating influences, flow in from the past social and cultural characteristics, from the environment, and from the genetic heritage of our species. Thus, this model argues that the present characteristics of a society are a product of three things: (1) the society's past, (2) the influences of the environment, and (3) the genetically based needs and abilities of the humans in it.

In turn, there are arrows flowing out of this box back to the environment and to the genetic heritage of our species. This not only indicates that present social arrangements *depend* on the environment (e.g., for edible plants, animals, water) and on our genetic heritage (e.g., resistance to disease), but that they have *effects* on them as well. When we farm land or domesticate animals, we change the environment; and x-rays, genetic engineering, and other technologies have the power to affect our genetic heritage.

This is the basic model of ecological-evolutionary theory, which provides the framework for all that follows in *Human Societies*.

IMPORTANT TERMS

macro/micro/sociology	scientific theory	falsifiable
hypothesis	empirical	millennium
ecological-evolutionary theory	global ecosystem	society
adaptive	cooperation	autonomy
biophysical/social/environment	information	genes
learning	threshold effect	myth
symbols/signals	genetic heritage	symbolic culture
modeling		

RECOMMENDED READING

1. *Science: Good, Bad and Bogus,* by Martin Gardner (Buffalo, NY: Prometheus, 1981). An interesting collection of essays by a highly respected science writer. As the title suggests, the essays explore and debunk a number of instances of bad, and in some cases fraudulent, science. His articles on nonhuman symbol use are of special interest.

2. *The Ape's Reflexion,* by Adrian Desmond (NY: Dial, 1979). An interesting nontechnical discussion of language use by apes and chimpanzees.

3. *The Language Instinct: How the Mind Creates Language,* by Steven Pinker (NY: Harper, 1994). A highly entertaining and informative exploration of how humans acquire and use language.

4. *Are We Unique? A Scientist Explores the Unparalleled Intelligence of the Human Mind,* by James Trefil (NY: Wiley, 1997). The title gives away the punch line of this short and very readable book.

5. *The Prehistory of the Mind: The Cognitive Origins of Art, Religion, and Science,* by Steven Mithen (London: Thames and Hudson, 1996). An archaeologist explores the origins of the modern human brain.

6. *The Symbolic Species: The Co-Evolution of Language and the Brain,* by Terrence W. Deacon (NY: Norton, 1997). A provocative and challenging theory of how the human brain and language became what they are today.

7. *The Social Cage: Human Nature and the Evolution of Society,* by Alexandra Mary-anski and Jonathan Turner (Stanford, CA: Stanford University, 1992). A detailed examination of the interplay and "fit" between human nature and various types of human societies, which comes to a very thought-provoking and counterintuitive conclusion about our biological "fit" with modern industrial societies.

8. *The Blank Slate: The Modern Denial of Human Nature,* by Steven Pinker (NY: Viking, 2002). A very readable and engaging reexamination of the "nature/nurture" debate.

9. *The Monkey in the Mirror: Essays on the Science of What Makes Us Human,* by Ian Tattersall (NY: Harcourt, 2002).

10. *The Discovery of Society,* 6th Edition, by Randall Collins and Michael Makowsky (NY: McGraw-Hill, 1998). A very readable introduction to the history of sociological thought, and the social theorists discussed in the excursus.

11. *Social Theory* 2004 (June) pp. 163–337, special issue edited by Bernice McNair Barnett. An exploration of ecological-evolutionary theory and Gerhard Lenski's life-long contributions to sociology and social theory by a diverse set of contemporary scholars.

QUIZ QUESTIONS

Fill-in-the-Blank

1. A basic feature of all sciences is _____.

2. The branch of sociology that focuses on *whole* societies is called _____.

3. A communication device whose form and meaning is *biologically* determined is called a/an _____.

4. A communication device whose form and meaning is *socially* determined is called a/an _____.

5. What two things must be true for a population of humans to be classified as a *society*? They must (1) _____ and (2) _____.

6. Everything *external* to a society but that can have an effect on it is called its _____.

7. The theory that guides *Human Societies* is called _____.

8. Two very different kinds of information that strongly affect human societies are (1) _____ and (2) _____.

9. The *process* whereby an animal acquires information that makes it possible for it to change its behavior and solve problems is called _____.

10. What primary purpose or function does *social organization* serve for animals that live in societies? _____

11. The two kinds of environments that confront human societies are (1) _____ and (2) _____.

12. The diagrams that illustrate the relationships that a theory says exist between things are called _____.

13. According to the model depicted in Figure 1.2 (p. 18), the social and cultural characteristics of human societies are shaped by three things: (1) _____, (2) _____, and (3) _____.

True or False

14. Social organization is an *adaptive* mechanism.

15. A good scientific theory should not be falsifiable.

16. Human beings are the only animals that live in societies.

17. Human beings are the only animals with the ability to *learn.*

18. Human beings are the only animals that have *created* symbol systems.

19. Human societies are part of the natural world.

Multiple Choice

20. Macrosociology is the branch of science that specializes in the study of human:
    a) interaction
    b) beings
    c) behavior
    d) societies
    e) intelligence

21. According to the book, social organization is:
    a) unnatural
    b) often harmful
    c) something only humans have developed
    d) all of the above
    e) none of the above

22. Which of the following is *not* part of the definition of "human society"?
    a) cooperation
    b) population
    c) political autonomy
    d) equality
    e) none of the above (all of these are part of the definition)

23. The theory advocated in *Human Societies* is called _____ theory.
    a) structural-functional
    b) social relativity
    c) ecological-evolutionary
    d) scientific-socialism
    e) none of the above

24. Which of the following has/have important effects on human societies according to the book?
    a) genes
    b) culture
    c) environment
    d) all of the above
    e) none of the above

25. According to the book, the environment:
    a) is outside of society
    b) has effects on society
    c) is both biophysical and social
    d) all of the above
    e) none of the above

26. According to *Human Societies*:
    a) symbols are the same as signals
    b) symbols have been invented by several nonhuman species (e.g., apes, chimpanzees)
    c) the meaning of a symbol is genetically determined
    d) all of the above
    e) none of the above

27. Different languages say "I love you" in different ways because the:
    a) meaning of a symbol is socially determined
    b) meaning of words is genetically determined
    c) genetic heritage of societies is so different
    d) different societies are in different environments
    e) none of the above

28. A unique feature of human societies is:
    a) learning
    b) symbolic culture
    c) cooperation
    d) social organization
    e) playing

29. A model is:
    a) a method of displaying cause and effect relationships
    b) a way of illustrating the relationships posited by a theory
    c) a visual diagram of what a theory says
    d) all of the above
    e) none of the above

Essay/Study Questions

30. What are *signals* and *symbols*? What are their important similarities and differences? What are their respective advantages and disadvantages for the animals that rely on them?

31. What are some of the important ways human beings are *similar* to other primates? What are some of the important ways they are *different*?

32. What did the experience of Helen Keller teach us about the "humanizing" effect of symbols?

33. If humans could not communicate, could they still build societies? Why or why not?

34. In what ways are human societies "adaptive"?

35. In what ways does living in groups *enhance* human abilities to learn and communicate?

36. How does ecological-evolutionary theory propose to explain the important characteristics of human societies?

NOTES

---

[1] *Millennia* are periods of 1,000 years (a single 1,000–year period would be a *millennium*). In contrast, *centuries* are periods of 100 years, and *decades* are periods of 10 years.

[2] The word *empirical* simply means based on sense perception (e.g., sight, touch, or hearing). Although telescopes, microscopes, and such things *extend* our senses, ultimately all scientific knowledge rests on perception of some kind. This source of knowledge is contrasted with mystical knowledge, imagination, or intuitive ideas, which are not accepted as evidence in the sciences.

[3] Strictly speaking, these terms have different meanings than they do in casual conversation. A hypothesis (hypothesis is singular, hypotheses is plural) is basically an "educated guess" that a researcher tries to test (i.e., find out if it is consistent with the best available evidence). In contrast, a theory is a set of propositions that *has been tested and confirmed.* Therefore, a hypothesis is *speculation,* but a theory isn't.

[4] This winnowing process is similar to that which is applied to college students. Although many are admitted, only those who pass tests and courses are retained and ultimately graduate. A single failure (test/course/semester) will not usually result in complete "rejection"—advising/counseling or probation may be recommended—but a continued pattern of failing will. One of the reasons employers are so interested in college *graduates* (even though the content of their major may not be directly relevant to the specific job they are hired to do) is that they, like successful scientific theories, have faced repeated tests and have passed the great majority of them.

[5] It is important to recognize that despite our species' unique genetic endowments, we share a number of important characteristics (to varying degrees) with other mammals and primates (e.g., see Table 1.1 on page 11).

[6] The most basic limitations on the information that can be stored and transmitted by symbols are those of its *users,* such as the limits of human memory. However, as we will see, even these limits are overcome with the inventions of writing and other systems that allow the storage and processing of information *outside* of people's heads.

2

Human Societies as Sociocultural Systems

CHAPTER SUMMARY

This chapter begins with a discussion of societies as sociocultural systems. It then presents a five-category system of classification of the components of human societies that will help organize the discussion of different types of societies in Chapters 5–14: (1) population, (2) culture, (3) material products, (4) social organization, and (5) social institutions. Each component is defined and discussed. The genetic constants and variables of human populations are discussed in some detail; components of culture are defined and discussed, as are the material products of culture and components of social structure. This is followed by discussion of social institutions and systems of social institutions. Kinship, the economy, the polity, religion, and education—the institutions that frame the discussion of the different types of societies—are identified as especially important. The concept of the "world system" of societies is introduced.

Chapter 2 introduces the vocabulary and framework that will be used in *Human Societies*. Many of these terms and concepts will be unfamiliar to you. My advice is that you go through the list of terms presented at the end of this chapter (and those at the ends of the chapters that follow) carefully and write out definitions of them. First, look up the definitions in the glossary (pages 351–358). A good college dictionary will provide definitions of any that are not in the glossary.[1]

It is critically important that you understand what a **system** is, and what a **sociocultural** system is. These terms will come up over and over again this semester. The key element of the concept **system** is that the parts are organized or *related* to one another. Thus a change in one part has effects on the other parts with which it is connected. In some systems the parts are very tightly connected (such as the gears of an automobile transmission); in others they are more loosely connected (such as weather systems). Insect societies are more tightly interrelated than are human societies. Calling human societies **sociocultural** systems emphasizes the fact that they are systems of social relations *and* systems of symbols and information (culture).

Five categories, (1) **population,** (2) **culture,** (3) **material products,** (4) **social organization,** and (5) **social institutions,** constitute the important elements of human societies and provide a framework for examining and comparing them. Understanding these categories, therefore, is important for understanding everything that follows. It is also important to keep in mind that since human societies are *systems,* these elements are *interrelated.* We break societies down into these components, not as a means of isolating them, but in order to see better how these elements are *interrelated* and to identify and trace *patterns* of change in them.

Population is subdivided into (a) **genetic constants,** (b) **genetic variables,** and (c) **demographic variables.** The **genetic constants** are those things that define us as a *species.* These are the biological characteristics that are basically the *same* in all human societies. Ironically, some of the things that are the *same* in all societies are responsible for making human societies so *different* from one another.

For instance, our abilities to **learn** and to invent **symbols** make it possible for us to develop bodies of information (i.e., **cultures**) that allow us to solve such basic problems as how to get food, make shelters, and raise children. We are not born with solutions to the basic problems we will confront; the solutions that are developed and retained will depend very much on the environment that our group confronts and its prior experiences with it.

Our common genetic heritage, therefore, enables us to adapt our behavior and social organization to the particular situation we are in. Groups in *different situations* will develop *different* patterns of behavior and organization. Thus the ability to use symbols and build cultures, which is *common* to all human populations, helps explain the great *diversity* of human societies.

In contrast, the common genetic heritage of many species of social insects produces *uniformity,* not diversity. Since the social *behavior* of insects is largely determined by their genes, insects of a given species, who share many of the same genes, will organize and behave in very similar ways. This dependence of behavior on genes also means that, unlike human societies, the societies of social insects do not change very much over time. In fact, the only way they *can* change significantly is if their genetic heritage changes, and, under normal conditions, this takes thousands or even millions of years to occur.

To say that we can adapt to different and changing situations does not mean that biology does not affect the way we act and the way we are organized. You should pay particular attention to the kinds of influences our biology has on us, and to the limits these influences put on the kinds of societies we are capable of developing and living in (pages 25–28).

It was once popularly thought that human beings were born as "blank slates" (*tabula rasa*) or "empty cabinets." This belief implied that children would become whatever they were raised to be. We now know this is not the case. Although no *specific forms* of behavior appear to be genetically programmed—human beings *do not* have instincts—our biological heritage does put limits on what we can do and how we can be organized socially.

Genetic variables are fascinating examples of how physical differences can develop when populations are isolated in very different climates. Even sometimes-deadly genetic characteristics, such as the "sickling cell," can develop and be passed on if, on balance, they provide an adaptive advantage.

As fascinating as they are, however, it is important to keep in mind the fact that the genetic differences between human populations are dwarfed by the similarities among them. We are a single species, *Homo sapiens sapiens,* and our underlying biological and genetic *similarities* greatly outweigh differences in our physical appearance.

As I noted earlier, and as the following chapters will demonstrate, these biological *similarities* are what make our behavior and social organization so *different,* not our biological *differences,* which are really rather superficial.

Demographic variables are variations in such things as the number of people in a society (population size), how closely they live to one another (population density), the relative numbers of males and females (sex ratio), the relative numbers of adults and children (age structure), and the rate at which people are born and die (birthrates and death rates).

As you will see in the following chapters, these things can vary quite markedly between societal types and over time, and when they do, they can have dramatic effects on
other features of society. In fact, **population growth** has been a major contributing cause
and consequence of virtually all fundamental social changes.

It is difficult to exaggerate the impact and importance of **symbolic culture**—
society's symbol systems and the information they contain (see pages 31–38). In fact, this
unique characteristic of human societies is the most important reason that human societies differ from one another.

The most basic symbol systems are **spoken language** and **body language. Written
language** and **numeral systems** are relatively recent inventions.

It is important to recognize that body language is a *symbol* system, not a system of
signals. The connections between body language gestures (head shaking, shoulder shrug-
ging, arm waving, etc.) and their "meaning" are *socially,* not genetically, determined.
Often the same physical gesture has a very different meaning in another culture (the same
way that the same "sound" or the same "word" has different meanings in different languages; e.g., see discussion of the sound "c" on page 15 of Chapter 1. If gestures were
truly signals, all *humans* would understand the gestures of all other *humans.* Instead,
countless misunderstandings and much embarrassment have resulted when individuals
from different cultures have encountered one another and assumed they could communicate by these means.

The development of **written language** has had a revolutionary impact on human societies. By overcoming the limits of human memory, it has enabled societies to amass large
bodies of useful information about a variety of topics and problems. Just think of all the
information there is in a *single* library, and keep in mind that as long as people can read,
this information is available to its users. Prior to writing, the only information available to a
group was that which its members could *remember.* In contrast, the overwhelming majority
of information in industrial societies is stored *outside* of people's heads—in libraries, files,
servers; on compact disks, flash drives and the like. In fact, a good deal of what you will
learn in college is *not information,* but how to *look for, access,* and *process* information.

Recognize also that much of the **information** in cultures is not simply *factual* (true
or false), but involves *judgments* and *values* (distinctions between what is good and bad).
The **ideology** of a society doesn't just offer an explanation of *why* things are the way they
are, but also tends to *justify* existing arrangements. **Ideologies** contain **beliefs, moral
values,** and **norms.**

As will become increasingly apparent in the chapters that follow, **technology** is one
of the most important parts of culture. It is defined on page 37. Notice that technology is
defined as *information.* Technology is *knowing how* to do, or make, something. When
you actually employ that knowledge to make something, the result is a **material product**
(technology + material resources). Thus the *knowledge* required to make a computer or to
grow corn is **technology;** the computer and the corn would be **material products of culture.** Tools are *not* technology; the **information** required to make them *is.*

Two of the most important **products of culture** are *energy* and *capital goods.* **Energy** is important because it sets the basic limit on what societies can *do.* All activities
require energy—moving people and things, building things, fighting wars, playing
games, even thinking. The amount of energy available to a society, thus, greatly affects
its ability to do things; the more energy it has available to it, the more things it can do.

Capital goods, things that are *needed* to make other things, are important not only because they affect the amount and types of valued goods that can be produced in a society, but
also because they are a major factor affecting the distribution of valued goods (i.e., social
inequality). In societies where everyone has free access to capital goods, there is very little

inequality. In societies where some individuals and groups *own* or *control* capital goods, those individuals and groups tend to dominate their society politically and economically.

Social organization is defined on page 38 as the network of relationships among members of a society. Without going into all the details, there are a few key points worth emphasizing. When we fill social **positions**, we are expected to act in certain ways and not in others. What we are expected to do, and in some cases can be punished for if we don't, is embodied in **social roles**. We have to *learn* how to fulfill the expectations associated with these roles, as well as the language and the lore of our society. This life-long process of learning is known as **the socialization process**.

In addition to this *horizontal* dimension of social organization (people may occupy different social positions, fulfill different roles, belong to different groups), there is also a *vertical* dimension. If social positions and roles are accorded different amounts of respect and social honor, and if different segments of the population have differing access to the valued resources in a society (e.g., power, privileges, and wealth), they can be described as constituting different **strata**[2] or **classes**.

All the different dimensions on which people can be ranked or judged unequal (e.g., wealth, income, power, respect, etc.), taken together, constitute a society's system of **stratification**. Among other ways, systems of stratification vary in the extent to which performing different social roles or belonging to different social groups affects one's access to valued social goods, the extent to which positions on different dimensions of inequality compound or offset one another, and in terms of the magnitude of the disparities that exist between people at the top and at the bottom of the system.

For instance, when the association between the horizontal and vertical dimensions is strong, members of different groups and people enacting different roles have substantially different access to the resources and rewards of society. This is clearly the case in agrarian societies, where lords are rich and privileged and peasants are not. In addition, when the associations between different dimensions of ranking are strongly related, then people and groups high on one dimension (e.g., power) are also high on others (e.g., income, wealth), and those low on one dimension are also low on the others. In such systems, inequality is *compounded* across dimensions of ranking. This too is clearly the case in most agrarian societies. Peasants lack not just power, but also wealth, income, education, and other privileges.

In other stratification systems, where the association across dimensions of inequality is lower, people's positions on different dimensions may vary independently, and, thus, may partially offset one another. A low position on some dimensions (e.g., wealth, income, political power) may be combined with relatively high positions on others (e.g., education, prestige).

The durable answers that develop in response to important and recurring problems confronting a society (e.g., raising children, resolving arguments, making decisions, etc.) are known as **social institutions**. They each consist of all four of the social elements already discussed: (1) **population**, (2) **culture**, (3) **material products**, and (4) **social organization**.

For instance, consider educational **institutions** in our own society (e.g., elementary, secondary, and higher education). They consist of (1) **population:** *people* involved in the process (e.g., people teaching and people attending classes), (2) **culture:** *information* about how to teach and the *information* to be taught, (3) **material products of culture:** the desks, buildings, pencils, computers, and the like, and finally (4) **social organization:** the roles and social organization of the institutions (e.g., teacher, student, school districts, classes, administrative hierarchy of authority).

The **social institutions** of a society also constitute a *system* (see Figure 2.2 on page 43). Therefore, what happens in one has effects on the others. In the case of the educational institutions just mentioned, not only would changes in the economy and the family affect educational institutions, but changes in educational institutions would, in turn, also have effects on the family and economy.

The chapter closes with a discussion of the **world system of societies**. This reminds us that societies are never completely isolated. Now, as we are increasingly aware, economic decisions made in Saudi Arabia, and China have affected the economy of the United States, and political decisions in Russia and Teheran, and moral issues raised in Africa, have affected the world. In part, this is a product of our better communication and greater *awareness* of the connections between societies; but, as we will see, it is also a result of the growing number and strength of international ties.

IMPORTANT TERMS

system	sociocultural	ecosystem
population	*tabula rasa*	genes
genetic constants	genetic variables	irony
demographic variables	culture	information
ideology	beliefs	moral values
norms	sanctions	customs
taboo	technology	metallurgy
material products	capital goods	roles
social organization	socialization process	strata
classes	primary groups	secondary groups
stratification	social institutions	
institutional systems	world system of societies	

RECOMMENDED READING

1. "Sociology and the Second Darwinian Revolution: A Metatheoretical Analysis," by Richard Machalek and Michael W. Martin (*Social Theory* 2004 pp. 455–476). Good overview of contemporary thinking on the interrelationship between human biology and social organization.

2. *Evolution and Human Origins,* by B. J. Williams (NY: Harper & Row, 1973). Explores the adaptive roles of some genetic variables in human populations.

3. *Evolution,* by Monroe W. Strickberger (Boston: Jones and Bartlett, 1990). A textbook on evolution, with chapters on the biology and evolution of humans.

4. *The History and Geography of Human Genes,* by L. Luca Cavalli-Sforza, Paolo Menozzi, and Albert Piazza (Princeton, NJ: Princeton University Press, 1994). A comprehensive summary of what these scholars and others have learned about the history and diffusion of various genes in human populations, complete with maps and tables.

5. *The Institutional Order: Economy, Kinship, Religion, Polity, Law, and Education in Evolutionary and Comparative Perspective,* by Jonathan Turner (NY: Addison-Wesley, 1997). An in-depth examination of the patterned institutional changes that have resulted from changing technologies and environments.

6. *The Social Cage: Human Nature and the Evolution of Society,* by Alexandra Mary-anski and Jonathan Turner (Stanford, CA: Stanford University, 1992).

7. *The Blank Slate: The Modern Denial of Human Nature,* by Steven Pinker (NY: Viking, 2002).

8. *The Symbolic Species: The Co-Evolution of Language and the Brain,* by Terrence W. Deacon (NY: Norton, 1997).

9. *The Monkey in the Mirror: Essays on the Science of What Makes Us Human,* by Ian Tattersall (NY: Harcourt, 2002).

10. *Anguished English* (NY: Doubleday, 1987); *Crazy English: The Ultimate Joy Ride Through Our Language* (NY: Pocket Books, 1989, 1990); and *The Miracle of Language* (NY: Pocket Books, 1991), by Richard Lederer. Three of my favorite explorations of the joys and pitfalls of communicating with language; be prepared to laugh.

QUIZ QUESTIONS

Fill-in-the-Blank

1. When the parts of something are *interrelated,* it is known as a/an _____.

2. The five basic components of human societies are (1) _____,
(2) _____, (3) _____, (4) _____, and (5) _____.

Classify each of the following items (3–13) on the basis of these five components:

3. a hammer

4. information on how to grow plants

5. the numbers of people in societies

6. social classes

7. birthrates

8. the *physical* ability to speak

9. religion

10. rules of behavior

11. the economy

12. differences in average body size and body shape in different populations of humans

13. a computer

14. Elements of genetic information that are the *same* in all human populations are known as genetic _____, whereas elements of genetic information that are *different* are known as genetic _____.

15. The biologically based human ability to create and use _____ is what makes culture possible.

16. Differences in such things as population size, density, birth and death rates are known as _____ variables.

17. Taken together, a society's symbol systems and the information they convey constitute that society's _____.

18. The process through which an infant learns to be a functioning adult member of society is called _____.

19. Information that is used to make sense of one's experiences and the organization of society is known as _____.

20. Things (material products) that are used to make other things are called _____.

21. Durable answers to important and persistent problems (e.g., raising children, settling disputes) are called _____.

22. The system of relationships among *societies* is called the _____.

23. The laws, regulations, and rules of a society are known as _____.

24. All of the dimensions of ranking or inequality in a society taken together constitute the society's system of _____.

True or False

25. Because of their genetic heritage, human beings are powerfully motivated to give the satisfaction of their own needs and desires a higher priority than they do the satisfaction of the needs and desires of others.

26. Human beings depend on society for survival.

27. Medieval Christianity is an example of a comprehensive ideology.

28. The tools and machines of a society are elements of technology.

29. A family is a secondary group.

30. The structure of the brain of modern humans reflects its evolutionary history.

31. Chimpanzees and apes have developed their own languages in the wild.

Multiple Choice

32. When the parts of something are interrelated, it is a:
    a) system
    b) mess
    c) society
    d) relative
    e) norm

33. Which of the following constitutes one of the five basic components of societies distinguished in the text?
    a) population
    b) social organization
    c) material products of culture
    d) all of the above
    e) none of the above

34. The belief that humans are "blank slates" at birth is called the _____ theory.
    a) *e pluribus unum*
    b) *tabula rasa*
    c) *post hoc ergo propter hoc*
    d) *caveat emptor*
    e) *carpe diem*

35. Which of the following is *not* a demographic variable?
    a) population size
    b) population density
    c) sex ratio
    d) birthrate
    e) body language

36. Differences in human physical attributes that have developed in populations as a result of prolonged exposure to very different biophysical environments are examples of:
    a) genetic constants
    b) genetic variables
    c) material products of culture
    d) body language
    e) demographic variables

37. Material products of culture that are used to make other things are called:
    a) capital goods
    b) technology
    c) institutions
    d) roles
    e) genetic variables

38. Cultural information that enables a society to use the material resources of its environment to satisfy human needs is called:
    a) social organization
    b) technology

c) material products of culture
d) norms
e) ideology

39. Rules of appropriate behavior in societies are called:
   a) norms
   b) strata
   c) technology
   d) genes
   e) systems

40. A society's symbol systems and the information they convey are called:
   a) a network
   b) culture
   c) social stratification
   d) a sacred cow
   e) an institutional system

41. Socialization is the term that denotes the process by which:
   a) the government acquires ownership of private industries
   b) an individual learns how to be a productive member of society
   c) people enjoy face-to-face interaction with others like themselves
   d) societies develop more advanced technologies
   e) none of the above

42. The system of beliefs, norms, and moral values that help a group to interpret its experience and order its social life is called a/an:
   a) sanction
   b) role
   c) ideology
   d) signal
   e) cherubim

43. Marvin Harris argues that the Hindu belief in the sacredness of cows is:
   a) adaptive
   b) wasteful
   c) impossible to understand or explain
   d) all of the above
   e) none of the above

44. The differences in social honor and prestige accorded different social roles are known as differences in social:
   a) status
   b) position
   c) function
   d) rewards
   e) none of the above

45. A segment of a population that occupies a similar position in regard to a basic social resource (e.g., wealth, income) constitutes a/an:
   a) primary group

b) secondary group
c) class
d) institution
e) network

46. The behavior that is expected/required of a person occupying a particular position in society is called a social _____.
    a) system
    b) institution
    c) role
    d) class
    e) group

47. Which of the following is *not* a component of social institutions?
    a) population
    b) culture
    c) material products of culture
    d) social organization
    e) environment

48. The system of relations among *societies* is called the _____ of societies.
    a) confederation
    b) amalgamation
    c) world system
    d) geopolitical condition
    e) united republic

Essay/Study Questions

49. Why is the concept of "system" important for the understanding of human societies?

50. Why are there so many different ways to say "I love you" in human societies?

51. Why might human societies be called systems of "antagonistic cooperation"?

52. What are some of the important genetic constants that shape human societies?

53. What are some of the features of culture that are found in *all* human societies?

54. Do nonhuman societies have cultures? Why or why not?

55. Give an example of an important social institution; tell how it incorporates elements of population, culture, material products, and social organization.

56. Why are human societies called *sociocultural* systems?

NOTES

[1] I strongly urge you to buy such a dictionary for yourself—you may, in fact, be required to buy one for an English course—but if you don't, the reference section of your college or public library will have one you can use.

[2] *Strata* are, quite simply, layers. A single layer is a *stratum*.

3

The Evolution of Human Societies

CHAPTER SUMMARY

The component processes of sociocultural evolution—continuity, innovation, and (intra- and inter-societal) selection—and the factors that affect them are first discussed individually. This is followed by an examination of their combined effects on long-term trends in societal development and characteristics of the world system of societies. An excursus comparing biological and sociocultural evolution follows.

As we noted in the first chapter of *Human Societies,* one of the remarkable things about human societies is their variability and propensity for change. Just consider the changes that have occurred in your society since you, or your parents, were children, or since the country was founded some 230 years ago. Even more dramatic are the changes that have occurred over the past 20,000 years. Twenty thousand years ago all societies were small and simple, and they managed to obtain what they needed to survive simply by hunting wild animals and gathering wild plants. Chapter 3 proposes an evolutionary model to explain how and why the world system of human societies has changed so dramatically over this time period.

Sociocultural evolution is the outcome of three fundamental processes: (1) **continuity,** (2) **innovation,** and (3) **selection.** Forces of continuity are conservative and act to keep things the way they are; forces of innovation create alternatives and promote change; and forces of selection ultimately determine which alternatives persist. Taking them in order, let's briefly consider each of these components of the evolutionary process.

A number of features of societies produce *resistance* to change. For instance, individuals and groups are often content to keep things the way they are, especially *if they seem to work.* We become accustomed to doing things a certain way, and, after a while, we follow the same pattern without even thinking about it.[1] In other cases, we are discouraged from doing something differently because violations of societal customs and norms may provoke ridicule and can even lead to punishment.

The *systemic* nature of societies and cultures is also an important factor fostering resistance to change. Because the elements of society are *interrelated,* changing one thing often entails changing many other things. Unless there is some compelling reason to change, most of these other systems and parts will generally *resist* being changed. Therefore, the more features of society that are affected, the *greater* the resistance to change is likely to be.[2]

There are three important kinds of **innovation** in societies—**diffusion, discovery, and invention.**[3] **Diffusion** occurs when an idea or element of one culture finds its way into another. A **discovery** is the addition of a *new* idea (e.g., finding a new metal) to a culture. In contrast, an **invention** is a *new combination* of *existing* ideas or cultural elements (e.g., making a telescope by putting glass lenses at both ends of a tube).

The quotations from the anthropologist Ralph Linton on page 50 clearly show the role of diffusion in enlarging the cultural store of information available to the members of modern societies. In fact, little of what we have or do was developed or invented in our own society.

The fact that a number of important **inventions** were made at about the same time by people working *independently* points to the important role that the amount and kinds of cultural information in a society play in affecting the likelihood of inventions. In fact, the frequency of simultaneous independent invention led one anthropologist, Leslie White, to conclude that if the information necessary for a useful invention exists in a culture, *it is only a matter of time before the invention is made.* Once the information is present, an invention can occur by chance or accident. This may be a bit extreme, even granting the number of important inventions that have occurred by accident, but it does call attention to the importance of the *size of the cultural store of information* for the likelihood of innovation and invention.

Another way to appreciate the importance of information is to examine Table 3.1 (page 49) and compare it to Figure 3.1 (page 52). Table 3.1 shows that as the amount of information in a culture increases, it rapidly *multiplies* the number of inventions (i.e., combinations of ideas) that are possible. Interestingly, if you were to plot the last column of Table 3.1 (the total number of possible inventions) by the first column (the number of ideas), it would look very much like Figure 3.1. As the number of ideas increased, the number of possible inventions would increase at a faster and faster rate.

Thus even if nothing else changed, the accumulation of information would tend to increase the *rate* of invention. However, when the information base of a society expands, other factors that affect the rate of change are likely to change as well. Therefore, if substantially more information should begin to accumulate in a society as a result of some key innovation (e.g., development of writing, improvements in transportation and communication technology that increase information flows within and between societies), the rate of innovation is likely to increase at an *accelerating* rate.[4]

Selection and **extinction** operate at two levels. **Selection** occurs *within* societies (**intrasocietal selection**) when individuals and groups choose among competing cultural traits and behaviors (e.g., deciding whether to use clay pottery or lead utensils in preparing food). The trait that continues can be said to have been selected "for," and the one that is abandoned is selected "against" or becomes extinct.

Selection also goes on *between* and *among* societies (**intersocietal selection**), such as when two societies compete for a territory or a resource. Such contact can lead to the disintegration, absorption, or conquest of one of the societies. The extinguished society would be said to have been selected "against." And if some types of societies are more likely to survive (have selective advantages) than others, there would be an increase in the relative number of societies of that type, and a decrease in the relative number of other types, over time.

The boxed insert on pages 54 and 55 of *Human Societies* poses an interesting "paradox" concerning changes in the world system of societies over the past 10,000 years;[5] namely, that although most *individual* societies did not change very much during their existence the *world system* of societies has changed dramatically.

How can this be the case? How can the *world system* of societies have changed so much when most *individual* societies did *not* change?

The answer is actually quite simple. If most of the societies that didn't change *disappeared* or became *extinct*,[6] and the few that did change *survived* and grew (in part by absorbing the smaller societies), then the two trends don't contradict one another. In fact, the two trends are perfectly consistent. The only way that some societies could have become *very large* is if many of the smaller ones disappeared or became part of larger ones.

This is illustrated with hypothetical data[7] in Table 3.2 on page 54—societies A and B grow in size, societies C and D do not change size, and societies E, F, G, H, I, and J become extinct by Time 4. If you express these as percentages, you will see that 80 percent of the societies either did not grow or became extinct, and only 20 percent of them grew. Nonetheless, despite the fact that most societies did *not* grow, the average size of societies in the *world system* of societies increased dramatically. The average size of societies at Time 1 was 100, but by Time 4 the "average" society had more than 1,000 members!

The paradox also illustrates a key element of the process of sociocultural evolution—namely, that it is the process of *selection* that produces *trends* in the world system of societies (e.g., on average they get larger, more powerful, more complex). Variation among, and change within, individual societies provide the *possibilities,* but it is the selection *among* societies that produces systematic trends. If larger societies are more likely to survive, and smaller societies less likely to survive, then, over time, (surviving) societies will, on average, be larger.

Subsistence technology is one of the important ways in which societies can differ and change, and it is one of the most important factors affecting selection. First and foremost, **subsistence technology** affects the amount of energy available to a society, and this, in turn, affects the number of people it can feed and the amount and the kinds of things it can do. As Figure 3.3 (page 58) shows, advances in subsistence technology (i.e., changes that *increase* the amount and kinds of energy available to a population) not only impact other important features of society and social organization, but also make advances in *other technologies* possible.

This is elaborated in Figure 3.2, on page 56, and Figure 3.4, on page 60. Figure 3.2 shows how technological advance, through its effects on other features of society, can lead to "selective advantage." Figure 3.4 shows how this effect on selection can produce (or, from another point of view, explain) major trends that have occurred in the world system of societies over the past 10,000 years or so the increasing size and complexity of human societies.

The excursus at the end of the chapter calls attention to the similarities and differences between biological and sociocultural evolution, and compares Lamarck's theory of biological evolution to Darwin's. Lamarck thought that the things that an animal *acquired by experience* (e.g., knowledge, big muscles) were passed on *biologically* to its offspring. Biologists have since established that this does not occur in reproduction; animals (including humans) do *not* pass on *acquired* abilities and characteristics genetically.[8]

Darwin's theory maintained that trends in the biological characteristics of a population over time occur if some characteristics increase the chances of survival and reproduction. Members of the population with the advantage are more likely to survive and reproduce, as are their offspring who inherit that characteristic. As a result, animals with that characteristic come to constitute an ever larger proportion of each generation.

Ironically, despite the fact that Lamarck was wrong about *biological* evolution, what he said has great relevance for *sociocultural* evolution. In **sociocultural evolution,** learned and acquired characteristics *are* passed on socially. This is one of the reasons that **sociocultural evolution** is so much *faster* than biological evolution.

IMPORTANT TERMS

biophysical	paradox	continuity
extinction	innovation	alteration
discovery	invention	diffusion
selection	intersocietal	subsistence
selective advantage	sociocultural evolution	fecundity
adaptive	nonadaptive	maladaptive
nomadic	feedback	information
"self-sustaining"	learning	evolution
functional equivalent		

RECOMMENDED READING

1. *Man's Way,* by Walter Goldschmidt (NY: Holt, Rinehart, and Winston, 1959). Still an excellent statement of technology's role in sociocultural evolution. Crisp formulation of many of the basic principles of ecological-evolutionary theory.

2. *Cultural Materialism* (NY: Random House, 1979); *Cannibals and Kings* (NY: Random House, 1977); and *Cows, Pigs, Wars, and Witches* (NY: Random House, 1974), all by Marvin Harris. The first book presents a comprehensive materialist theory of sociocultural evolution; the other two provide detailed analyses of how certain cultural features of societies first emerged and the "functions" they fulfill for their populations.

3. *Social Change,* by William F. Ogburn (NY: Viking, 1950). Classic analysis of social change within individual societies. The discussion of inventions and discoveries is especially valuable.

4. *The Discoverers: A History of Man's Search to Know His World and Himself,* by Daniel J. Boorstin (NY: Random House, 1983). A very readable and entertaining account of fundamental discoveries in the realms of (1) time, (2) the earth and the seas, (3) nature, and (4) society. Truly enlightening.

5. *Ancient Inventions,* by Peter James and Nick Thorpe (NY: Ballantine, 1994). A comprehensive, well-illustrated compendium of inventions and discoveries prior to 1492 A.D.

6. *Plagues and Peoples,* by William McNeill (Garden City, NY: Anchor, 1976). Very carefully and convincingly traces the "coevolution" of human societies and human diseases.

7. *Evolution,* by Monroe Strickberger (Boston: Jones and Bartlett, 1990). A very good college-level text on evolution with some pertinent observations on humans and human societies.

8. *The Illustrated Origin of the Species,* by Richard Leakey (London: Rainbird, 1979). Good abridgement of the classic by Darwin.

9. *The Blind Watchmaker,* by Richard Dawkins (NY: Norton, 1986). Provides an excellent discussion of how *cumulative selection* and random variation can produce incredibly complex structures.

10. *Of Moths and Men: The Untold Story of Science and the Peppered Moth,* by Judith Hopper (NY: Norton, 2002). An entertaining and intriguing behind-the-scenes account of the drama and characters who produced the now-controversial research that provided critical support for Darwin's arguments concerning the role of natural selection in biological evolution. For a view more supportive of the research, see "Moonshine: Why the Peppered Moth Remains an Icon of Evolution," by Matt Young and Ian Musgrave, *Skeptical Inquirer* 2005 (March–April), pp. 23–28).

11. *The Ghost Map: The Story of London's Most Terrifying Epidemic—and How It Changed Science, Cities, and the Modern World,* by Steven Johnson (New York: Riverhead Books (Penguin Group), 2006). The fascinating, and perhaps cautionary, tale of how conventional wisdom and scientific consensus concerning the causes of a cholera epidemic in mid 19th century London were overturned by the stubborn persistence of one man with a radical theory and another with on-the-ground experience and eye for detail.

12. *Energy and Society,* by William F. Cottrell (New York: McGraw-Hill, 1955). A classic statement of the impact of energy on societies that stands the test of time. In addition, Chapter 1 of his *Technology, Man, and Progress* (Columbus, OH: Merrill, 1972) provides a valuable discussion of the role of technological innovation in the larger process of social change.

QUIZ QUESTIONS

Fill-in-the-Blank

1. Ten thousand years ago there were _____ people on the earth living in (how many?) _____ societies.

2. Today there are _____ people on earth living in (how many?) _____ societies.

3. The "great paradox" of societal evolution is posed by the apparent contradiction between the fact that the *world system* of societies has _____ over the past 10,000 years or so, despite the fact that most *individual* societies _____.

4. The three basic components of sociocultural evolution are _____, _____ , and _____.

5. When one society adopts a feature (e.g., a belief, a tool) from another, this is called _____.

6. Relatively unimportant changes, such as changes in hem lengths, hairstyles, or the width of men's ties, are called _____.

7. According to the book, finding the cause of polio was an example of a/an _____ , whereas making the first light bulb was an example of a/an _____.

8. Changes in _____ have the most powerful impact on societal development and change.

9. Starting with the most important, list as many of the things that affect the *rate* of innovation in societies as you can:

    a._____
    b._____
    c._____
    d._____
    e._____
    f._____
    g._____

10. According to the example in the book, if an illness causes a decline in appetite and this leads to a *worsening* of the illness, _____ feedback has occurred.

11. The long-term outcome of the interplay between forces of continuity, innovation, and selection is called _____.

12. Things that are *learned* are passed on in _____ evolution, but they are not passed on in _____ evolution.

True or False

13. Ten thousand years ago the average society had about 300 people living in it.

14. The most common fate of human societies has been extinction.

15. Every item added to the cultural information of a society *multiplies* the number of inventions that are possible.

16. There are no important similarities between biological and sociocultural evolution.

17. There are more than 6 billion people alive today.

18. The reason that there are more inventions in industrial societies than there were in hunting-gathering societies is that people are more intelligent today than they were 10,000 years ago.

19. The automobile is a good example of a discovery.

20. The forces of continuity promote change in societies.

21. Symbols play a role in sociocultural evolution that is similar to the role played by genes in biological evolution.

22. Paradoxically, the systemic nature of human societies is something that offers resistance to change, but it can also help spread, throughout a society, the effects of changes that do occur.

23. Human fecundity is a force that promotes innovation and change.

24. Intersocietal selection occurs when people choose one cultural trait, such as the automobile, over another, such as the horse and buggy.

Multiple Choice

25. Which of the following statements is/are true about human societies over the past 10,000 years?
    a) Technological advance has occurred in the world system of societies.
    b) Most individual human societies have become extinct.
    c) Technological advance has been rare among individual societies.
    d) all of the above
    e) none of the above

26. Which of the following generally *increases* the rate of innovation?
    a) population growth
    b) a stable environment
    c) isolation
    d) all of the above
    e) none of the above

27. Which of the following does *not* generally promote continuity?
    a) socialization
    b) the biological process of aging
    c) a stable environment
    d) contact with other societies
    e) a strong commitment to tradition

28. A new combination of existing cultural elements is called a/an:
    a) discovery
    b) alteration
    c) diffusion
    d) extinction
    e) invention

29. When useful information from one society finds its way into another society, _____ has occurred.
    a) cultural infection
    b) diffusion

      c) discovery
      d) selection
      e) invention

30. Which of the following has the greatest impact on the process of societal growth and development in human societies?
      a) the average intelligence of the population (a genetic variable)
      b) the attitude of the population toward change and innovation
      c) advances in subsistence technology
      d) changes in ideology
      e) developments in religion

31. Intersocietal selection occurs when _____ become extinct.
      a) ideas
      b) animals
      c) symbol systems
      d) societies
      e) populations

32. According to the book, the process of intersocietal selection has favored societies that are:
      a) stable
      b) innovative
      c) small
      d) resistant to change
      e) harmonious

33. Which of the following is/are involved in the process of sociocultural evolution?
      a) continuity
      b) innovation
      c) selection
      d) all of the above
      e) none of the above

34. Which of the following is *not* a cause of innovation in human societies?
      a) human needs
      b) chance
      c) a growing store of cultural information
      d) a changing environment
      e) none of the above (all of these are causes of innovation)

35. The simultaneous, independent invention/discovery of things like calculus, sunspots, and the telephone illustrates the importance of _____ in the process of sociocultural innovation.
      a) intelligence and creativity
      b) hard work and perseverance
      c) the existing store of cultural information
      d) genius
      e) an ideology that favors change and novelty

36. Over the past 900 to 1,000 years, the rate of technological innovation has generally:
    a) declined
    b) been relatively constant
    c) increased dramatically
    d) gone up and down in several cycles of long duration
    e) been random

37. The process of change and development in human societies that results from the interplay of forces of continuity, innovation, and selection is called:
    a) sociocultural evolution
    b) the march of human progress
    c) manifest destiny
    d) the bootstrap phenomenon
    e) feedback

38. Intersocietal selection has generally favored societies with:
    a) strong religious beliefs
    b) ideologies that oppose innovation and change
    c) large stores of technological information
    d) weak military institutions
    e) small populations and simple social organizations

39. Which of the following is/are true of both biological and sociocultural evolution?
    a) Both involve systems of coded information.
    b) Continuity and change are present in both.
    c) Variation and selection play a role in both.
    d) all of the above
    e) none of the above

40. How do biological and sociocultural evolution differ?
    a) Learned information is passed on socioculturally but not genetically.
    b) Isolation speeds up change in biological evolution but slows it down in sociocultural evolution.
    c) Biological evolution is generally slower than sociocultural evolution.
    d) all of the above
    e) none of the above

Essay/Study Questions

41. How has the evolution/development of *individual societies* been different from the evolution/development of the *world system of societies*? Why is this difference called a paradox?

42. Why has subsistence technology had such an important influence on the character of societies and the process of social change?

43. How do the forces of *continuity, innovation,* and *selection* produce systematic trends in the world system of societies?

44. What are some of the most important trends that have occurred in the world system of societies over the past 10,000 years?

45. Why has the rate of innovation accelerated so rapidly in the past 1,000 years?

46. How are changes in subsistence technology linked to changes in other important features of societies?

47. What *types* of societies have been favored by intersocietal selection over the past 10,000 years? What trends has this produced in the world system of societies?

48. According to the excursus, what are some of the most important *similarities* between biological and sociocultural evolution? What are some of the most important *differences*?

NOTES

[1] Although we are quick to recognize problems with "bad" habits, we often forget how much time and effort "good" habits save us on a daily basis. The effectiveness of habit is called to our attention only when something *interferes* with our normal routine. Getting ready for work or school, for instance, takes longer, and we are more likely to forget something we need, when our normal schedule is interrupted or changed.

[2] On the other hand, if a fundamental feature of society (e.g., subsistence technology) *does change,* it will put tremendous pressure on *many* other features of that society to change.

[3] A fourth kind, **alteration** (e.g., fashion's hem lengths, lapel widths), is distinguished by its general *lack of social importance.*

[4] These elements have all increased so dramatically in modern industrial societies that some have questioned whether we as a *species* can adapt to such a dizzying rate of fundamental change. Alvin Toffler referred to the hurricane of change that swirls through industrial societies as "future shock."

[5] A paradox exists when two things that appear to contradict one another, are *both* true.

[6] It is important to keep in mind that *autonomy* is a key element of the definition of society. A society ceases to exist—becomes extinct—if it loses its autonomy (e.g., is conquered or absorbed by another society). Societal extinction, therefore, does not imply that all or most of a society's population die, or that its cultural information is lost. It simply means that it is no longer an independent and self-directing system.

[7] It is worth emphasizing that these are *not* data on actual societies. They have been artificially constructed to provide a concrete example of the abstract principles that explain the "paradox." Thus they *illustrate* rather than *test* theoretical principles.

[8] They pass on genetic potentials and predispositions, but they do not pass on the effects of their own experiences. The body of genetic information that a parent can pass on to offspring is fixed at the *parent's conception.* (A minor exception to this is the possibility that a parent's genetic information can be damaged by chemicals or radiation in the parent's lifetime.)

4

Types of Human Societies

CHAPTER SUMMARY

The chapter opens with discussion of the two most important influences on human societies—technology and environment. First, the taxonomy of types of human societies, based on **subsistence technology**, is presented (Table 4.1 displays the criteria of classification). Figure 4.1 indicates the level of technological advance (information and energy) of the different types of societies, and shows common paths of development. Historical eras, the periods in which the various types were dominant in the world system of societies, are demarcated, and then data on a variety of social characteristics are presented to demonstrate the utility of the taxonomy of societies and ecological-evolutionary theory. Clear and supportive differences in the (1) size of societies, (2) permanence of settlements, (3) societal complexity, and (4) ideology are found by societal type. The chapter closes with a discussion of the limitations of the typology and a disavowal of technological determinism.

If sociology is the *scientific* study of human societies, and the essence of science is *systematic comparison* (see Chapter 1), we need a system of classification (typology or taxonomy) for ordering observations and organizing comparisons if we are to do sociology. Such a system should enable us to place societies that share important similarities in the *same* category and to place societies that are different from one another in *different* categories. Furthermore, the rules (criteria) of classification in such a system should be simple and objective.[1]

Since ecological-evolutionary theory argues that **subsistence technology** is the single most important factor affecting social organization and development, in *Human Societies* we use indicators of subsistence technology to classify societies.[2] Table 4.1 (page 64) shows the indicators that will be used and the rules for using them. Application of the rules distinguishes six *primary* types of societies—hunting and gathering, simple horticultural, advanced horticultural, simple agrarian, advanced agrarian, and industrial. These societal types are the focus of most of the rest of the book (Chapters 5–7, and 9–13).[3]

A society is classified in terms of the way it gets *most* of its food (i.e., its "dominant mode of subsistence"). Societies that obtain most of their food by foraging for wild plants and killing wild animals (with spears and/or bows and arrows) are **hunting and gathering**. Table 4.1 shows that it is characterized by the *absence* of all the identified traits. A society that *cultivates* most of its food (in *gardens*) using digging sticks or hoes, but *does not use plows,* is **horticultural**. **Advanced horticultural** societies have *metal* tools and weapons; **simple horticultural** do not. Metallurgy, the technology for making metals and forming them into tools, is present in the former but absent in the latter. A society that *cultivates* most of its food (in *fields*) using *plows* is **agrarian**. **Advanced agrarian** societies have *iron* tools and weapons; **simple agrarian** do not.[4] Finally, **industrial** societies are distinguished from all the others by their dependence on nonliving ("inanimate") sources of energy in the production of their subsistence.[5]

45

Following the discussion of the system of classification are some illustrations of its use. It is important to keep in mind that in these illustrations and in the comparisons that follow, each comparison is a test both of the system of classification and of the theory upon which it is based. To the extent that societies that are similar are grouped together, and societies that are different are separated, the system of classification is shown to be useful, and indirectly, the theory it is based on is shown to be effective. In contrast, if the system of classification did *not* work, both the typology and the theory that generated it would be suspect.

The second most important factor affecting social organization and development is the **environment**. The environment greatly affects the *potential* for technological development, and it affects the *kinds* of development that are likely to occur.

Figure 4.1 on page 64 orders the different types of societies in terms of their levels of technological advance—those toward the bottom of the figure (e.g., hunting and gathering, fishing) have harnessed relatively smaller amounts of energy per person than those toward the top (e.g., agrarian, industrial)—and shows common paths of development. The societies in the main column on the left of the figure have been more numerous and they have occupied a wide variety of environments. Those on the right have been much rarer and they have been restricted to more "specialized" social and biophysical environments.[6]

As some societies developed more advanced technologies, the circumstances of less advanced societies generally changed for the worse. For, now, in addition to possible competition and conflict with societies having similar subsistence technologies, there was the possibility of competition with larger, more powerful societies (see Figure 4.2 on page 67). It is thus important to know what types of societies were the most advanced in different periods (eras) of history. These dates are discussed, and there is a summary of the eras on pages 67–68.[7]

To demonstrate the usefulness of this system of categorizing societies, a number of tables and figures follow. Each is designed to show the impact of **subsistence technology** on an important dimension of society. As I noted earlier, if key characteristics of societies vary systematically by categories of **subsistence technology**, then both the classification system (typology) and **ecological-evolutionary theory** from which it is derived receive empirical support.

Does the size of societies vary systematically by **subsistence technology**? Table 4.2 (page 70) shows the median size of societies that depend on different **subsistence technologies**.[8] Clearly, the sizes of societies are strongly associated with their "dominant mode of subsistence." For instance, simple horticultural societies are *40 times* the size of hunting-gathering societies, and industrial societies are *10,000 times* the size of simple horticultural societies![9]

Also, data discussed on page 70 show—not surprisingly—that 94 percent of the societies that *cultivate* their food (horticultural and agrarian) are *sedentary* (settled in one place), and 90 percent of the hunters and gatherers are *nomadic* (move their campsites periodically).

Are technologically more advanced societies more *complex*? Table 4.3 and Figure 4.3 on page 71 suggest they are. The first shows that occupational specialization is more common in more advanced societies, and the second shows that more advanced societies have more *complex* systems of stratification (i.e., their populations are distributed across a greater number of distinct statuses).[10]

In less advanced societies, families are more likely to produce all of their subsistence needs (e.g., housing, clothing, pottery, etc.) *themselves,* rather than specializing in the production of some things (e.g., tools, food) and *exchanging* them for others (e.g., housing, clothes). Increased specialization and the resulting increase in exchange both serve to make more advanced societies more complex.

Figure 4.3 shows that this specialization and increased exchange also tend to make systems of stratification more complex. In less advanced societies, people are either pretty much the same in terms of wealth, power, and privileges, or fall into relatively few status categories (e.g., slave, freeman), whereas in more advanced societies, there are a greater variety of statuses occupied by people (e.g., peasant, merchant, servant, scribe, soldier, ruler).

Up to this point, all of the examples have involved dimensions of **population** and **social organization**. But does subsistence technology also affect nonmaterial aspects of social life, such as **ideology**? Figure 4.4 (page 72) indicates it does. The structure of religious beliefs varies systematically by subsistence technology. Whereas belief in a "creator God concerned with the moral conduct of humans" is found in only a very few hunting-gathering and horticultural societies, it is found in the majority (64 percent) of agrarian societies.[11]

This brief examination of the effects of **subsistence technology** is a preview of what follows in *Human Societies*. Chapters 5, 6, and 7 more closely examine hunting-gathering, horticultural, and agrarian societies, respectively.[12] Chapter 8 focuses on "environmentally specialized" societies (fishing, herding, maritime), and Chapters 9–14 focus on industrializing and industrial societies. Chapter 4 closes with a discussion of the *limitations* of subsistence technology as an explanatory variable. To say, as ecological-evolutionary theory does, that subsistence technology is the *single* most important factor affecting societies is not to say that it is the *only* factor that affects societies. There is variation among societies in the same category of subsistence technology, and subsistence technology does not *determine* all other features of societies. It may shape, and constrain, but it does not *determine*.

Finally, it is important to recognize the fact that societies may vary in the *degree* to which particular attributes are present. For instance, they may be *more or less* democratic, making it difficult or impossible to make a categorical statement that a society is or isn't a "democracy." Furthermore, the relationships between social characteristics are *probabilistic* (see the earlier discussion on "How to Read Tables" in the "Introduction" of the *Primer and Guide*). For example, although industrialization greatly increases the *probability* or the *likelihood* of a representative form of government, it does not ensure that industrial societies are everywhere or always democratic (e.g., see the excursus to Chapter 14, pages 321–322).

The excursus presents a brief history of sociology and a discussion of the conceptual and theoretical differences among contemporary sociologists, and it closes with a comparison of (macro)sociology with other social sciences.

IMPORTANT TERMS

typology	taxonomy	cultivation
subsistence technology	foraging	inanimate
metallurgy	plows	horticulture
hybrids	environmentally specialized	vertical
agriculture	maritime	mean
horizontal	median	variables
determinism	probabilistic	

RECOMMENDED READING

1. *Cannibals and Kings* (NY: Random House, 1977); and *Cows, Pigs, Wars, and Witches* (NY: Random House, 1974), both by Marvin Harris. These volumes offer many interesting examples of the influence of material factors on the nonmaterial components of culture.

2. *The Elementary Forms of the Religious Life,* by Émile Durkheim (NY: Free Press, 1965 [1915]). Classic sociological explanation of the origin of the "sacred" and the social functions of religion and religious ceremonies.

3. *Birth of the Gods,* by Guy Swanson (Ann Arbor, MI: University of Michigan Press, 1964). Detailed test of hypotheses advanced or suggested by Durkheim's work.

4. *The Evolution of Human Societies,* by Allen Johnson and Timothy Earle (Stanford, CA: Stanford University Press, 1987). An excellent source on the evolution and adaptation of human societies by two eminent anthropologists.

5. *Man's Way,* by Walter Goldschmidt (NY: Holt Rinehart and Winston, 1959). Chapter 6 is a good introduction to societal taxonomy. Chapter 4, on "The Mechanisms of Social Evolution," is also very relevant to the issues raised in this chapter.

QUIZ QUESTIONS

Fill-in-the-Blank

1. A society that relies on two or more technologies for its basic subsistence is called a/an _____ society.

2. The system for classifying societies (taxonomy) in *Human Societies* is based on _____.

3. Fishing, herding, and maritime societies are _____ societies.

4. The technology for making metals is called _____.

5. The two most basic causes of fundamental differences between societies are differences in their _____ and differences in their _____.

6. What type of society was the most technologically advanced in 200 b.c.?_____.

7. What type of society cultivated fields with iron plows? _____.

8. What type of society was the most technologically advanced in 15,000 B.C.? _____.

9. What type of society cultivated food in gardens and used stone tools? _____

10. What type of society was the most advanced in 6500 B.C.?

    _____

11. What type of society was the most advanced in 3500 B.C.?

    _____

12. What is the *oldest* type of society? _____

13. What is the *newest* type of society? _____

14. Which was larger, the average agrarian or the average horticultural society?

    _____

True or False

15. Hunting and gathering societies generally have permanent settlements.

16. Most horticultural and agrarian societies are nomadic.

17. Ecological-evolutionary theory argues that technology explains everything about societies.

18. Dependence on inanimate energy sources characterizes industrial societies.

19. A key reason for developing a typology of societies is that it enables us to make systematic comparisons between types of societies.

20. Advanced horticultural societies are examples of environmentally specialized societies.

21. The industrial era began in 1000 A.D.

22. The horticultural era ended about 10,000 to 8000 B.C. (i.e., 10,000 to 12,000 years ago).

23. The horticultural era began when the first horticultural societies developed.

24. None of the hunting and gathering societies we have information on had "craft specialization."

25. The average (median) size of an industrial society is 5,250.

26. Although not one of the hunting-gathering societies had a complex status system, *every* industrial society does.

27. Subsistence technology is the single most important force that makes societies different from one another.

28. Ecological-evolutionary theory is probabilistic.

Multiple Choice

29. Information on which of the following is used to classify societies?
    a) plant cultivation
    b) metallurgy
    c) plow
    d) iron
    e) all of the above

30. A society that relies on the plow for most of its subsistence is classified as a/an
    _____ society.
    a) hunting and gathering
    b) horticultural
    c) agrarian
    d) all of the above
    e) none of the above

31. Which of the following types of society is *most* likely to believe in a "creator-God concerned with the moral conduct of humans"?
    a) hunting and gathering
    b) simple horticultural
    c) advanced horticultural
    d) agrarian
    e) maritime

32. Which of the following types of society is *least* likely to believe in a "creator-God concerned with the moral conduct of humans"?
    a) hunting and gathering
    b) simple horticultural
    c) advanced horticultural
    d) agrarian
    e) maritime

33. Which of the following does *not* vary across categories of subsistence technology?
    a) societal size
    b) religious beliefs
    c) societal complexity
    d) all of the above (none of these varies by societal type)
    e) none of the above (all of these vary by societal type)

34. What type of society uses iron tools and weapons?
    a) hunting and gathering
    b) simple horticultural
    c) advanced horticultural
    d) simple agrarian
    e) advanced agrarian

35. What type of society cultivates most of its food in gardens (without plows) and uses metal tools and weapons?
    a) hunting and gathering

b) simple horticultural
c) advanced horticultural
d) simple agrarian
e) advanced agrarian

36. What type of society was the most technologically advanced in 20,000 B.C.?
    a) hunting and gathering
    b) simple horticultural
    c) advanced horticultural
    d) simple agrarian
    e) advanced agrarian

37. What year marks the beginning of the agrarian era?
    a) 20,000 B.C.
    b) 10,000 B.C.
    c) 8000 B.C.
    d) 3000 B.C.
    e) 1000 A.D.

38. What year marks the end of the agrarian era?
    a) 15,000 B.C.
    b) 5000 B.C.
    c) 3000 B.C.
    d) 2000 B.C.
    e) 1800 A.D.

39. What type of society does *not* cultivate most of its food?
    a) hunting and gathering
    b) simple horticultural
    c) advanced horticultural
    d) simple agrarian
    e) advanced agrarian

40. What type of society relies on inanimate sources of energy to produce most of its subsistence?
    a) hunting and gathering
    b) horticultural
    c) agrarian
    d) herding
    e) industrial

Essay/Study Questions

41. Why are societies classified in terms of their subsistence technologies?

42. What information would you need to classify a society in terms of its "dominant mode of subsistence"? Illustrate with some examples.

43. How have differences in biophysical environment affected societies and their *potential* for technological advance?

44. How do such things as the permanence of community settlements, the size of societies, the division of labor and complexity of stratification, and the structure of religious beliefs vary across categories of subsistence technology? Why are these differences noteworthy?

45. What is "technological determinism"? Why is it rejected?

NOTES

[1] *Criteria* are rules for judging or classifying something; a single rule is a *criterion*. That the system of classification (criteria) should be "objective" simply means that the information necessary to classify a case is openly observable, and any two observers following the classification rules will put a given case in the *same* category.

[2] Since we cannot *directly* and objectively measure technology and energy in any but the most advanced industrial societies, we must base our classification of most societies on the **material products** or observable results of **subsistence technology**. This is especially true for societies that must be classified based on historical records or physical traces and artifacts.

[3] The "environmentally specialized" societies—fishing, herding, and maritime—are discussed in Chapter 8, and the hybrids—industrializing horticultural, and industrializing agrarian societies—are discussed in Chapter 14.

[4] Iron is distinguished from other metals because, while iron *ore* is more plentiful, *iron* is (technologically) more difficult to make and to form into tools and/or weapons than earlier-discovered metals and alloys (e.g., copper, bronze). Societies that develop this technology, therefore, not only gain a "superior" material for making tools and weapons, but also have a more abundant one.

[5] Notice that the presence of these attributes is *cumulative*. For example, societies that use *plows* also have *metallurgy* and *cultivate* plants. Even in advanced industrial societies people continue to hunt animals, gather plants (e.g., mushrooms, berries), and garden, and they continue to use plows and iron implements in addition to depending on inanimate energy sources.

[6] For example, fishing societies have been restricted (biophysically) to sea coasts and inland waterways, and maritime societies have been restricted (biophysically) to areas with access to deep ports and (socially) to times and places where societies had surplus goods that could be transported and traded.

[7] Some further context is provided by Figure 6.1 (page 107), which gives dates and locations for the domestication of a variety of important plants and animals.

[8] As the boxed insert on page 69 indicates, the *median* is a measure of central tendency (what is common or typical for a set of observations) that is not greatly affected by extreme values ("outliers").

[9] The sizes of fishing and of herding (communities and) societies are discussed in more detail in Chapter 8 of *Human Societies* (see page 179).

[10] Occupational specialization is an aspect of the *horizontal* dimension, and status complexity is an aspect of the *vertical* dimension of **social organization** discussed in Chapter 2 of *Human Societies* and the *Primer and Guide*.

[11] Such a belief is found in virtually all advanced industrial societies.

[12] "Respectively" simply means in that order—that is, in the same order as they were just discussed.

5

Hunting and Gathering Societies

CHAPTER SUMMARY

The chapter begins with a review of the archaeological evidence on hunting and gathering so cieties during the hunting and gathering era (100,000 to 8000 B.C.). Table 5.1 identifies the major technological innovations that have occurred over the past 4,000,000 years, and traces the dramatic acceleration in the rate of change in human societies in recent millennia. Table 5.2 shows the dramatic acceleration in the rate of growth in world population during this era. The chapter then turns to the ethnographic evidence gathered in studies of hunting and gathering societies in the modern era. It discusses the technology of hunting-gathering societies and the basic features of their population (size, density, birth and death rates), nomadic lifestyle, social structure, social institutions (kinship, economy, polity, stratification, religion, education, and arts and leisure), and formation of tribal ties through societal fissioning. This is followed by a comparison of the archaeological and ethnographic data. A model of "limited development" in hunting-and-gathering societies is presented in Figure 5.3, showing how the key common characteristics of these societies flow from the technology of hunting and gathering and work together to maintain a low rate of technological and societal innovation. The chapter closes with a discussion of the possibility that this type of society, which has served our species well for so many millennia, is not likely to survive into the twenty-first century.

Although hunting and gathering has been practiced in hominid societies for millions of years, the first *completely modern humans* probably did not emerge until sometime in the past 100,000 to 150,000 years. Hunting and gathering, or foraging, thus was *inherited* by humans from their prehuman ancestors.[1] Once humans just like us (*Homo sapiens sapiens*) did develop, however, their enhanced ability to use **symbols** allowed **cultural** adaptation to replace biological adaptation as the primary means by which hominids adjusted to, and coped with, their environments.

As a result, there have been many dramatic and fundamental changes in **symbolic cultures** since then, but only minor and superficial changes in human **biology**.[2] It is not possible to pinpoint the exact date when the first truly human hominids walked the earth, but there is a very strong consensus that *there has been no fundamental biological change in humans over the past 40,000 years.*

Thus, when we talk about societies 10,000, 20,000, or even 40,000 years ago, we are talking about people who are biologically *indistinguishable from us.* They were just as intelligent, just as emotional, and just as articulate as we are. Differences between their societies and ours, therefore, *cannot* be explained by biological differences between us and them. Other things must account for these differences, and subsistence technology is one of the most important of those "other things."

Hunting and gathering is a very effective means of providing the necessities of life if societies are small, widely dispersed, and have extensive territory open to them for foraging and hunting. As Table 5.3 (page 86) shows, the *greater* the reliance on hunting and gathering, the *smaller* the society; or, looking at it from the other side, the *smaller* the society is, the *less* it must supplement its subsistence with cultivation and other technologies.[3] Table 6.1 in the next chapter (page 110) of *Human Societies* also shows that hunting and gathering societies have much lower population densities than do societies that *cultivate* most of their subsistence.[4] In fact, the average population density of hunting-gathering societies (0.6 persons per square mile) is *less than* the current population densities of Wyoming (5.3 persons per square mile) and Alaska (1.2 persons per square mile).

Hunting and gathering also requires that societies be *nomadic.* In Chapter 4 (page 70), we noted that 90 percent of hunting and gathering societies were nomadic, in contrast to only 6 percent of horticultural and agrarian societies. The reason is that since they are not growing their own plants or raising their own livestock, hunters and gatherers must go to where the plants and animals are growing and raising themselves.

Do they find this periodic moving troublesome or annoying? In a word, no. Since they move (generally every few weeks or months) from places where resources have been depleted to places where they are abundant, and also leave behind garbage and other sanitation problems, moving is something they look forward to and enjoy.

Many of us find moving—particularly *temporary* moves—an inconvenience and annoyance for two reasons. First, we have to pack and carry a large and continually growing number of possessions we have accumulated. Second, when we move, we often have to leave loved ones behind, and face the prospect of having to make new friends.

Neither of these is a serious problem in hunting and gathering societies. First, because they move so frequently, they don't accumulate many possessions. They don't have such things as furniture, stoves and refrigerators, closets full of clothes, CD collections, DVDs, and books. Moreover, since housing is temporary, it is generally easy to construct with readily available materials, and the food-producing technology is either portable (e.g., bows and arrows, spears) or readily replaceable (e.g., digging sticks).[5] Second, since the *entire* society moves, painful separations do not occur.

The basic organizing principle of hunting and gathering societies is **kinship**. This means that *obligations* and *responsibilities* between people are based primarily on *kinship.* We will have much more to say about kinship systems in the next chapter; but for now, we should note that kinship is not simply another word for *biology.*

Kinship systems are systems of *social* relationships, and they differ from biological relationships in many important ways. In some cases, people who *are* related biologically *are not* related by kinship. In such systems, despite the fact that the people may recognize a biological tie, they do not have *specific and enforceable social responsibilities for one another.* In some cases, people *not* related by biology *may be* related by "fictitious" ties of kinship.

This is the reason that anthropologists and sociologists pay such careful attention to kinship in these societies. *It* is the system that *structures* behavior and responsibilities between people, and *it* is the primary social resource people have for dealing with economic, social, and political problems. Although people in these societies have friends, and friends may help one another, only people related by kinship are *obligated* to help or assist one another in specific ways. Furthermore, even though children are raised to be self-reliant (see Table 5.5 on page 98), in the absence of governments, police, courts, armies, churches, hospitals, and the like, kinship groups are relied on to defend members' interests, resolve disputes, distribute resources, and do the countless other things that individuals cannot do for themselves.

The practice of **exogamy**, which requires that individuals marry someone from another kinship group, helps to extend economic and political ties *across* kinship groups, just as the intermarriages of the various royal families in European history helped to establish economic and political alliances among *societies.*

Work in hunting and gathering societies is divided and assigned on the basis of age and sex. Women do the majority of gathering—up to 80 percent in some societies—and have primary responsibility for the care of young children. Men do the hunting.[6] Children learn their adult roles by accompanying their parents and gradually assuming increasing responsibilities as they grow and mature.

Hunting and gathering societies do not have anything we would recognize as a "government." This is because, being small aggregations of people who know one another, they can make decisions that affect the group *informally.* Moreover, if individuals or families disagree with the majority decision, they are generally free to leave the group and take up residence with relatives/friends in neighboring societies, or, if there are enough of them to constitute a self-sufficient group, to strike out on their own.

Although most hunting and gathering societies have a "headman," the position and the rewards it commands are largely "symbolic." Headmen may *influence* others, but they cannot *command* them (see Figure 5.2 on page 93). If the headman generally makes wise decisions, his advice will be followed; if he does not, he will be ignored. Furthermore, since being a headman is a part-time role and headmen must provide for their own families, they generally *work harder* than the average member of their society. It is only in technologically more advanced societies, where leaders can demand tribute and taxes, that substantial material rewards accrue to leaders.

The fact that the basic technology and resources of the society are open and available to everyone is one of the reasons individuals and groups cannot accumulate substantial power in these societies. As Table 5.4 (page 95) shows, land ownership is rare or absent in these societies. Societies are accustomed to hunting in certain territories and will defend their *collective* right to use that land, but no *individuals* or *families* can claim an exclusive right to it. As a result, no individuals or groups are in a position to use control of this resource to gain control or power over those who need access to it for survival.

To the typical hunter-gatherer, ownership of plants and animals *is* something of concern, but it is not an issue of contention until a plant is picked or an animal killed—then (sometimes quite elaborate) rules of ownership and distribution come into play. In contrast, since land cannot be eaten or worn, it is generally not something they are concerned with "owning."[7]

Having few possessions and little basis for gaining leverage over one another, there is little **stratification** in hunting and gathering societies. When people have something of value, kinship and social pressure generally force them to share it.

Thus, the only real differences between people are differences in **prestige**—good hunters are respected for their skills, good storytellers and comedians for their ability to amuse and entertain, *shaman* for their apparent abilities to ward off evil spirits and heal the sick, and the elderly for their accumulated wisdom and practical knowledge.

Many of these features of hunting and gathering societies evoke an image of a peaceful, harmonious, idyllic life—especially if we find ourselves in large, impersonal cities confronting cold, bureaucratic organizations—but it is important to avoid *romanticizing* hunting and gathering societies. True, they consist largely of related individuals and friends, and therefore are characterized by warm, intimate ties between people. But, as with all families and groups of friends, they are subject to the disruptive influences of jealousy, envy, and conflict.

A common, and often effective, remedy to such conflicts is simply to separate the individuals or families that are in conflict. Because people have friends and relatives in neighboring societies (encouraged by **exogamy**), it is usually relatively easy to leave one society and to go live in another.

Should such arrangements fail, however—given the fact that all adult males are armed and skilled in the arts of hunting and killing—conflicts are very likely to be deadly.

One study indicated that hunters and gatherers may have had homicide rates in the range of 29 to 42 per 100,000 population.[8] For comparison, recent figures show that the United States, one of the most violent industrial societies, had a rate of about 6.0 per 100,000 population (down from 10.2 in 1980); New York City had a rate of 6.6, Los Angeles 12.6, Chicago 15.6, and Philadelphia 25.6.

Only some of the most violent U.S. cities—such as Baltimore with a murder rate of 42.0, Detroit with a rate of 41.4, Saint Louis with a rate of 37.9, and Washington, D.C., with a rate of 35.4—had rates as high, or higher, than those the study found in hunting and gathering societies. These are sobering statistics. Nonetheless, as we will show in the next chapter of *Human Societies* ("Technological Advance but Moral Regress?" pages 134–135), there is evidence that horticultural societies have even *higher* homicide rates than hunting and gathering societies.

Animism, the most common type of religion in hunting and gathering societies, maintains that spirits inhabit and animate virtually all things—animals, clouds, forests, streams, rocks, and humans. This implies that success in hunting, favorable weather, and cures for illness may be obtained if the responsible spirit is appropriately flattered, appeased, bribed, cajoled, tricked, or frightened. Thus, ironically, in societies with very little technological capacity to affect their environment or subsistence, there is often the belief that virtually everything—even the weather—is subject to human influence.

However, Table 5.6 (page 99) provides an additional insight into life in these societies. It shows that games of *strategy* are not found in them. This suggests that people in these societies don't feel they can consistently *control* the outcomes of their endeavors. Too many uncontrollable factors affect the supply of game and plants—the animating spirits, though potentially subject to human influence, are fickle and capricious—and hunting is too unpredictable to give people a sense that what they plan or do *determines* the success or failure of their actions.[9]

Finally, as we noted in our hypothetical photo album in Chapter 1 of *Human Societies,* innovation and change were limited in hunting-gathering societies. Thousands of years passed without fundamental technological changes occurring (remember Table 5.1 on page 81). One reason for this is the fact that people have little incentive to change if *what they are doing is working,* and as long as populations were small and societies were widely dispersed, hunting and gathering worked quite well.

However, as Figure 5.3 (page 102) illustrates, there were a number of additional factors that inhibited fundamental change in these societies. In fact, as we will see in more detail in the next chapter, it was probably only after population growth, increasing population density, and environmental change made hunting and gathering much less effective that technological change and plant cultivation became more common. As Table 5.2 (page 85) shows, population growth rates, although still low by modern standards, accelerated dramatically toward the end of the hunting and gathering era.

IMPORTANT TERMS

hominid	genus	nomadism
sympathetic magic	language	exogamy
ethnography	polygyny	monogamy
archaeology	kinship	solidarity
Homo sapiens sapiens	terrestrial	omnivore
carnivore	infanticide	idyllic
nuclear/extended families	animism	shaman
polity	headman	private property
socialization	tribe	archaeology
ethnography	ceremony	ritual
Paleolithic	Mesolithic	Neolithic
!Kung San	Ona	spear thrower

RECOMMENDED READINGS

If you would like to read more about prehistoric and contemporary hunting and gathering societies, I would suggest the following paperback books:

1. *The Harmless People,* by Elizabeth Marshall Thomas (NY: Random House, 1959).

2. *The Forest People,* by Colin Turnbull (Garden City, NY: Doubleday, 1961).

3. *The Hunters,* by Elman Service (Englewood Cliffs, NJ: Prentice-Hall, 1966).

4. *The Emergence of Man,* by John Pfeiffer (NY: McGraw-Hill, 1977).

5. *The Stone Age Hunters,* by Grahame Clark (NY: McGraw-Hill, 1967).

6. *The Hunting Peoples,* by Carleton Coon (Boston: Little Brown, 1971).

In addition, informative chapters on a variety of hunting and gathering societies can be found in:

7. *Our Primitive Contemporaries,* by George Peter Murdock (NY: Macmillan, 1934).

8. *Profiles in Ethnology,* by Elman Service (NY: Harper & Row, 1971).

9. *Peoples of Africa,* edited by James Gibbs (NY: Holt, Rinehart and Winston, 1965).

QUIZ QUESTIONS

Fill-in-the-Blank

1. _____ are members of the biological family that includes modern humans and their immediate predecessors.

2. The biological family *Hominidae* (our ancestors) probably split off from the ancestors of apes and chimpanzees about _____ years ago.

3. Cultural evolution replaced biological evolution as the primary means by which hominids adapted to their environment about _____ years ago.

4. The largest prehistoric hunting and gathering settlements had about _____ people in them.

5. In 8000 B.C. (about 10,000 years ago), there were about _____ humans on the earth.

6. In hunting and gathering societies, social organization (i.e., the structure of obligations and responsibilities between people) is usually based on _____.

7. The religious belief that all things are inhabited and guided by "spirits" is known as _____.

8. An individual who has a special ability to affect these "spirits" is known as a/an _____.

9. Among modern hunting and gathering societies, which would be larger: a society that relies on hunting and gathering for 50 percent of its subsistence, or one that relies on hunting and gathering for 90 percent of its subsistence? _____

10. A group of people who speak a distinctive language, share a common culture, have a distinctive name, but are members of separate, autonomous societies would be called a _____.

True or False

11. Chimpanzees and apes are *hominids*.

12. *Hominids* are omnivorous.

13. Only *Homo sapiens sapiens* (modern humans) bury their dead, and they started doing so less than 10,000 years ago.

14. Most hunting and gathering societies consisted of a single autonomous community.

15. The average hunting and gathering society had fewer than 50 members.

16. Women were big-game hunters in some hunting and gathering societies.

17. The headman and his police had considerable power in the typical hunting and gathering society.

18. Private ownership of land was rare or absent in hunting and gathering societies.

19. In hunting and gathering societies, children are raised to be obedient.

20. Because they are nomadic, hunting and gathering societies generally do not have any form of music.

21. Most hunting and gathering societies do not have games of chance.

22. Most families in hunting and gathering societies were polygynous.

23. Most large settlements of hunting and gathering societies were temporary.

24. A tribe is more of a *cultural* than a *social* entity.

25. There are almost no similarities between the prehistorical hunting and gathering societies described by archaeologists and modern hunting and gathering societies described by ethnographers.

26. Soon hunting and gathering societies may be extinct.

Multiple Choice

27. A spear thrower is:
    a) one type of warrior in hunting and gathering societies
    b) the most prestigious occupation in hunting and gathering societies
    c) the most feared enemy one can have in a hunting and gathering society
    d) a device that increases the speed and distance a spear can be thrown
    e) none of the above

28. The _____ was probably the most important innovation in weapons made during the hunting and gathering era.
    a) bow and arrow
    b) spear
    c) knife
    d) net
    e) none of the above

29. The belief that you can affect things by manipulating images or pictures of them is known as:
    a) ethnocentrism
    b) sympathetic magic
    c) technological determinism
    d) ecology
    e) humanism

30. Which of the following is *not* true of the "typical" hunting and gathering society?
    a) It is nomadic.
    b) It practices infanticide.
    c) It permits polygyny.
    d) It believes in animism.
    e) It is sedentary.

31. The requirement that one marry a member of a different kinship group is called:
    a) monogamy
    b) exogamy
    c) polygyny
    d) polygamy
    e) none of the above

32. The division of labor in hunting and gathering societies is usually based on:
    a) talent and ambition
    b) age and sex
    c) education and training
    d) interests and abilities
    e) none of the above

33. If an individual in a hunting and gathering society has a problem that he or she cannot solve for him/herself, who or what can s/he turn to for help?
    a) the government
    b) the tribal council of elders
    c) the headman
    d) his/her kinship group
    e) social workers

34. Stratification in hunting and gathering societies consists primarily of differences in:
    a) wealth
    b) power
    c) education
    d) prestige
    e) income

35. Which of the following would you *not* expect to find in a "typical" hunting and gathering society?
    a) religion
    b) art
    c) music
    d) intelligent people
    e) police

36. Which of the following is typical or common in hunting and gathering societies?
    a) a headman with substantial power
    b) private ownership of land
    c) games of strategy
    d) women hunters
    e) none of the above

37. Which of the following is the basic principle of organization in hunting and gathering societies?
    a) fear
    b) power
    c) bureaucracy

      d) kinship
      e) ethnocentrism

38. According to the model at the end of Chapter 5 (Figure 5.3, page 102), which of the following is/are (a) reason(s) that the rate of innovation was so *low* in hunting and gathering societies?
      a) They had a limited store of information.
      b) They were highly stratified.
      c) They had a highly developed division of labor.
      d) The people in them weren't very intelligent.
      e) all of the above

39. Another word for a *medicine man* in hunting and gathering societies is:
      a) headman
      b) shaman
      c) spear thrower
      d) chief
      e) doctorman

Essay/Study Questions

40. Describe the behavior of the members (men, women, boys, and girls) of a hunting-gathering society from the time they arrive at a new campsite until they abandon it for a new one.

41. Why were women not the hunters in hunting and gathering societies?

42. Why was periodic moving (nomadism) *not* considered a problem in these societies?

43. Why was the rate of innovation so low in hunting and gathering societies?

44. How did hunters and gatherers settle disputes and make political decisions? How did they treat illness? Practice their religion?

45. Why was kinship so important in hunting and gathering societies?

46. What can games tell us about life in a society?

NOTES

[1] Although the tools and techniques are not the same, hunting and gatherings is also still practiced by many nonhuman primates.

[2] To see one aspect of this, note the *differences* in the rates of innovation among prehuman and human societies, and the *acceleration* in the rate of innovation over the past 100,000 years shown in Table 5.1 on page 81.

[3] We saw earlier that the average size of hunting and gathering societies was 40 (see Table 4.2 on page 70 of *Human Societies*).

[4] Thus the acceleration in population growth revealed in Table 5.2 (page 85) is a key suspect in the process that led to the adoption of plant cultivation and the domestication of animals. We will examine this possibility more closely in Chapter 6.

[5] Social critics often complain about the fact that we are a "disposable" society. Rather than keep and maintain things, we throw them away and get replacements. Critics thus suggest that our "garbage problems" are a result of a *change in our behavior,* and imply, by contrast, that people in simple societies were neater and more frugal. Nothing could be further from the truth. Hunters and gatherers rarely kept anything after they used it—knives, bows, bags, "canteens," and the like were notable exceptions—and they certainly didn't worry about treating their sewage! Why do our garbage and sewage constitute such a serious problem whereas theirs didn't? There are basically two reasons: (1) the numbers of people involved, and (2) the *kinds* and *amounts* of things being thrown away. Remember that the average hunting and gathering society had only about 40 members, whereas industrial societies, on average, currently have about 10.5 *million* members (see Table 4.2 on page 70 of *Human Societies*). The populations of industrial societies are also much more concentrated. On average, there are more than 300 people per square mile in contemporary industrial societies, compared to *less than 1* per square mile (0.6) in hunting and gathering societies. Furthermore, the kinds of things we throw away don't decompose as readily. Milk containers, for instance, may last *thousands* of years. In contrast, the garbage of hunters-gatherers decomposes or "biodegrades" in a few weeks or months, and some of their "garbage," such as plant seeds and pits, may actually help to *replenish* and to *concentrate* their food resources. For a graphic description of some of the sanitation problems caused by the increasing concentration of sedentary populations in agrarian societies, see pages 151–152 of *Human Societies.*

[6] In some hunting and gathering societies, such as the Mbuti pygmies, women and children participate in the hunt by making noise and driving game into nets where they are killed by men. However, as the boxed insert "Why Were Women Not the Hunters?" on page 92, shows there are a number of reasons why women were not the hunters.

[7] This sets the stage for one of the many conflicting cultural views that have led to misunderstandings and violence between societies practicing different subsistence technologies. When agriculturalists "bought" land from foraging societies (often for something that had little value for them), they expected to be able to restrict access and use of it—for example, to clear it, fence it in, and cultivate it. The foraging societies that "sold" the land, however, still expected to be able to hunt, fish, and gather on it. Each probably felt they were getting something for virtually nothing in the deal. When each acted on its expectation—the agriculturalists fenced in the land, planted crops, and grazed domesticated animals, and the hunter-gatherers continued to "hunt" the animals and gather the plants that grew in the fenced areas—however, the response of the other to this activity was seen as a puzzling betrayal, and resentment, anger, mistrust, and violence often followed.

[8] Bruce Knauft's article, "Reconsidering Violence in Simple Societies," was in *Current Anthropology,* August–October 1987, Volume 28, pages 457–500.

[9] To see how games may be revealing, consider the fact that Monopoly is one of the most popular games in our (capitalist) society. To us it makes perfect sense and is "fun" for someone to end up with all the wealth by bankrupting his or her friends. However, to someone raised in a society where sharing is a way of life, and where the respect someone receives is based on how much s/he *gives away,* such a game would be unimaginable. Accumulating possessions at the expense of one's fellows would engender embarrassment and shame, not pleasure and pride.

6

Horticultural Societies

CHAPTER SUMMARY

This chapter begins with a discussion of the reasons *why* the first horticultural societies emerged some 10,000 to 12,000 years ago in southwest Asia. Growth in population, and climate change—"global warming"—apparently led to intensification of hunting and gathering, and "feedback" from this intensification ultimately forced societies to begin *cultivating* plants they had previously gathered, and to start raising animals they had previously hunted. After a brief discussion of the technology of slash-and-burn horticulture, simple horticultural societies are examined. Discussion of the prehistoric, simple horticultural societies of Asia and Europe is followed by discussion of simple horticultural societies in the modern era. Then, advanced horticultural societies are examined. Discussion of advanced horticultural societies of the past, in Asia and Europe, is followed by discussion of advanced horticultural societies in the modern era. A boxed insert "Horticulture in the New World" then considers (simple) horticultural societies of the New World, since having developed horticulture independently, they constitute an independent test of ecological-evolutionary theory. Finally, the key features and dominant trends in horticultural societies are placed in theoretical perspective. As the model depicted in Figure 6.6 (page 133) shows, this new subsistence technology made it *possible* for societies to produce a stable economic surplus, and, when they did, it gave rise to increased population size and density, a higher incidence of warfare, the first urban communities, concentration of political power, increases in the division of labor, inequality, changes in religion, and more. The chapter is followed by a brief excursus on the origins and inadequacies of racialist theories of social development.

The hunting and gathering era came to an end some 10,000 to 12,000 years ago when humans began to depend on food they were producing for themselves for most of their subsistence. Humans had domesticated plants and animals (see Figure 6.1 on page 107). Ironically, in the process, humans also *domesticated themselves.* Now they would have to stay "home" and tend these plants and animals rather than moving about and living off the land. This change would have dramatic effects on almost every feature of human life. It was quite literally a *revolution* in human societies and human existence.[1]

We are well aware of many of the positive features of this revolution—plants and animals would now grow where and when people wanted them to, and material wealth and occupational specialization would increase. Less obvious are some of the negative features—work would be harder and more routine; there would be greater inequality, including systems of slavery; conflicts and wars would become more frequent and more deadly; and problems with waste, sanitation, and vermin would become more serious.[2]

Given the rewarding features of hunting and gathering, and the less desirable features of horticulture, it is not surprising that the shift to a sedentary horticultural life appears to have been resisted. Hominids had been affecting the supply and distribution of plants and animals since they first developed, and the shift from gathering to cultivating plants was gradual and probably unplanned. However, it was only when the combination of increasing human population, changing climate, and decreasing supply of hunted animals made hunting and gathering ineffective that societies first began to rely on horticulture for *most* of their subsistence.

Once foraging societies began to intensify their hunting and gathering, they could easily be pushed to further intensify and ultimately change their mode of subsistence. This is because although intensification may have solved problems of food shortages in the *short run,* it did so only by making long-term shortages *worse.* Thus, hunters and gatherers could be forced to raise animals they were hunting, and grow plants they were gathering, even though it was much more drudgery and provided a less satisfying lifestyle.

The simplest and most basic form of horticulture is called *slash-and-burn* or *swidden* cultivation.[3] As the name implies, trees and shrubbery are simply cut, allowed to dry, and then burned. Seeds or cuttings are then planted right in the ashes. Since a plow doesn't have to be pulled across the land, there is no need to clear stumps from the garden. Different plants (e.g., plantains, tobacco, etc.) are planted in irregular patches among the debris and stumps (e.g., see photo on page 108). In fact, the ashes from the trees and shrubs actually help to fertilize the soil that is being cultivated. Thus, the gardens of horticulturalists more closely resemble patchwork quilts than they do the regular geometrical shapes that we associate with agriculture. Furthermore, although cultivating one's subsistence may require more work than does foraging in an abundant environment, by many estimates horticulture is more *energy efficient* than is industrial agriculture.[4]

The only problem is that it requires much land. Since a given plot can be cultivated for only a few years and must then be abandoned for fifteen to twenty years so the trees can grow back, every family must have access to an area that is four or five times the area that is under cultivation at any given time.[5] If, lacking this much land, they are forced to return to an abandoned area before it is completely reforested, it will require more work and it will produce less food. Thus if their populations continue to grow, at some point they will be forced to intensify their efforts and to develop and adopt technological changes (e.g., hoes to replace digging sticks), and ultimately, perhaps to abandon horticulture (e.g., see the illustration on page 138). We will have more to say about this in the next chapter.[6] Horticulture can support larger, more densely concentrated populations than could hunting and gathering. As Table 4.2 (page 70) shows, on average, simple horticultural societies had 1,500 members, and advanced horticultural more than 5,000; Table 6.1 (page 110) shows that their population densities were 13.8 and 42.7 per square mile, respectively. They are also more likely to be sedentary—whereas only 10 percent of hunters-gatherers had sedentary communities, more than 90 percent of horticultural societies have sedentary communities. On a darker side, they also could support more extended and more deadly conflicts (see the boxed insert, "Technological Advance but Moral Regress?" on pages 134–35). Table 6.4 (page 118) shows that warfare was "perpetual" or "common" in only 27 percent of hunting and gathering societies, in contrast to 60 percent of simple horticultural societies and 82 percent of advanced horticultural societies.[7]

Homicide rates in horticultural societies were also quite high. According to one study, they may have been as high as 400 or 800 per 100,000 population.[8] *This is 50 to 100 times the rate for the United States as a whole, and about 10 times the homicide rate of its most violent cities![9]*

Many of the mechanisms that were used to defuse conflicts within and between hunting and gathering societies were not possible or were ineffective in larger, more sedentary populations.

Horticulture and the increase in warfare also produced a dramatic increase in the incidence of slavery. In fact, some form of slavery is found in *almost every advanced horticultural society we have knowledge of!* Figure 6.5 (page 126) shows that 83 percent of advanced horticultural societies practice slavery in contrast to 45 percent of agrarian, 15 percent of simple agrarian, and 11 percent of hunters-gatherers. The technological advantage of metal weapons coupled with the fact that horticulture made slavery *economically viable* (i.e., unarmed adults could be controlled and used to cultivate gardens) was especially conducive to the institution of slavery.[10]

Increased warfare also gave rise to systems of trophy taking (e.g., scalps, shrunken heads, etc.; e.g., see the photo on page 120) and conquest. Single communities lost autonomy either because they were conquered and absorbed into other societies, or because they formed confederations in response to the threat of conquest. In some cases, warfare may also have increased rates of female infanticide.[11]

The development of a stable economic surplus increased occupational specialization and social complexity. Since horticulturalists had the *potential* to produce more food than they or their families needed for survival, it was possible for some people to specialize in occupations and activities other than food production (e.g., warrior, priest, politician, toolmaker, etc.). All that had to be added was an *incentive* to make this potential an actuality. A number of military and religious leaders produced such incentives. As a result, professional armies, religious elites, and governments developed in a number of advanced horticultural societies, as did spectacular religious monuments (e.g., see photo on page 130), defensive structures (e.g., see photo of the Great Wall on page 124), and other structures that required large labor forces and massive supplies of materials.

Kinship continued to be an important feature of social organization in horticultural societies. Individuals still depended very much on their kinship group as a mutual aid system; the kinship group often controlled access to cultivatable land, and, in order to make them more reliable and controllable, many rulers built their administrations around kinship and key relatives.

One interesting and *unusual* feature of kinship in horticultural societies is the relatively high incidence of **matrilineality** (see page 116). This high incidence is possibly connected to the visible importance of women in food production. Table 6.2 (on page 115) shows that food cultivation is primarily a female responsibility in 39 percent of horticultural societies compared to only 8 percent of agrarian; Table 6.3 (on page 116) shows that the greater the contribution of plant cultivation to subsistence in horticultural societies, the greater the likelihood that kinship is matrilineal.[12]

Another *unusual* feature of horticultural societies is the very high incidence of ancestor worship. Figure 6.3 (page 116) shows that ancestor worship is present in the great majority of horticultural societies (71 percent of simple and 82 percent of advanced), but in only a small minority of other types (17 percent of hunting and gathering and 27 percent of agrarian societies).

Chapter 6 ends with an excursus on "Race, Environment, and Societal Development." It considers the attempts that have been made from time to time to explain technological differences among societies as being the result of biological or genetic differences among their populations. These racist or racialist theories have focused on the fact that differences in development have often been associated with differences in *physical appearance*. The inference that is made from this is that both are the result of the same cause—racial or genetic differences among the populations.

Such explanations are plausible if one considers only a single historical era. For instance, in the contemporary world, Western societies, peopled by light-skinned Europeans and their offspring, are technologically and economically more highly developed than are most of those in Asia, the Middle East, and Africa. One might conclude from this particular pattern of peoples and development that relative levels of development are caused by, or explained by, *biological differences* in the populations of these societies and regions.

The problems inherent in such explanations become immediately apparent, however, when additional information and a wider time frame is considered. First, the distributions of peoples and relative levels of development have not always been what they are today. As we have just seen, horticulture emerged first in the Middle East. In the next chapter, we will see that agriculture and what we now call "civilization" also first emerged there. Thus, an area and people who in one era were on the "cutting edge" of technological development are on its margins in another. In addition, it is also the case that advanced civilizations flourished in Asia and Africa at a time when most Europeans were still practicing hunting and gathering.

Thus, the particular rank ordering of development in world regions in one era rarely, if ever, corresponds to that of another era. The same populations that are in societies at the forefront of development in one era are often in the "underdeveloped" or "Third World" societies of another.

Furthermore, there are often simpler explanations—differences in soil, rainfall, indigenous diseases—for why certain developments (e.g., plow agriculture) are unlikely in specific environments or conditions, whereas others (e.g., industrialization) are not.

Finally, if biology (race) were the explanation of differences in societal development, then fundamental changes in development would both require and reflect significant biological changes in the populations of societies. The problem with this is that, although there is good reason to expect that it would take a *minimum* of 25,000 to 250,000 years for significant biological changes to occur in human populations, *the technological developments and social changes we are considering occurred in a span of less than 10,000 years.*[13]

Clearly, the hypothesis that differences in levels of societal development can be accounted for by biological or genetic differences among populations has been refuted. As a result, racist or racialist theories of development have been discredited and abandoned by social scientists.

IMPORTANT TERMS

horticulture	domestication	Neolithic
swidden cultivation	obsidian	bitumen
slash-and-burn	smelting	bronze
alloy	kiln	unilinear
economic surplus	theocracy	Old World
multicommunity	New World	radiocarbon dating
clans	matrilineal	slavery
ceremonial cannibalism	retainers	state
ancestor worship	artisan	metallurgy
hereditary nobility	regress	female infanticide
priest	cannibalism	indigenous
racist/racialist theory		

RECOMMENDED READING

If you would like to read more about the development of horticulture and horticultural societies, I would suggest the following:

1. *The Emergence of Society,* by John Pfeiffer (NY: McGraw-Hill, 1977). Chapter 3 is especially informative regarding the shift to horticulture, and Chapter 4 provides an eye-opening discussion of the incidence of violence and homicide in simple societies.

2. *Cannibals and Kings,* by Marvin Harris (NY: Random House, 1977). Chapter 3 provides a popular statement of an interesting aspect of the explanation of the origins of horticulture, and Chapter 7 offers an interesting discussion of the origins of the state and coercive political systems.

3. *War before Civilization: The Myth of the Peaceful Savage,* by Lawrence H. Keeley (NY: Oxford University Press, 1997). An archaeologist explores the causes, the virulence, and the frequency of armed conflict between human groups in pre-state societies. See also: "Toward an Ecological-Evolutionary Theory of Incidence of Warfare in Preindustrial Societies," by Patrick D. Nolan (*Sociological Theory* 2003: 18–30.)

4. *Writing: The Story of Alphabets and Scripts,* by Georges Jean (NY: Henry N. Abrams, 1992); and *Numbers: The Universal Language,* by Denis Guedj (NY: Henry N. Abrams, 1997). Two beautifully illustrated and well-written paperbacks on the origins and development of these important symbol systems.

5. *The Ancient Sun Kingdoms of the Americas,* by Victor von Hagen (Cleveland: World, 1961). An excellent introduction to the Incas, Aztecs, and Maya. Very well written.

6. *Yanomamo: The Fierce People,* by Napoleon Chagnon (NY: Holt, Rinehart, and Winston, 1983); and *Into the Heart: One Man's Pursuit of Love and Knowledge Among the Yanomamo,* by Kenneth Good (with David Chanoff) (NY: Simon and Schuster, 1991). Something of a *Yin* and *Yang* of Yanomamo ethnographies; two very different accounts of the societies of these South American horticulturalists.

7. *The Conquest of New Spain,* by Bernal Diaz (Baltimore: Penguin, 1963). An eyewitness account of the first Spanish contact with, and ultimate conquest of, the Aztecs. Relates the fascination, fear, and horror experienced by one of Cortes's soldiers. See also Chapter 6 in *Carnage and Culture: Landmark Battles in the Rise of Western Power,* by Victor Davis Hanson (NY: Doubleday, 2001).

8. *Cortes and the Downfall of the Aztec Empire: A Study in a Conflict of Cultures,* by Jon Manchip White (NY: Carroll & Graf, 1989). This very readable and entertaining book reveals as much about the economic and social motivations of Hernan Cortes as it does about Moctezuma and Aztec society. It is, therefore, relevant to the next chapter too.

9. *Dugum Dani,* by Karl Heider (Chicago: Aldine, 1970). Excellent account of the culture of these New Guinean horticulturalists (subjects of the film "Dead Birds"), especially their beliefs about spirits of the dead and the need for war.

10. *Man Makes Himself,* by V. Gordon Childe (NY: Mentor, 1951). Chapters 5 and 6 are classic accounts of the impact of horticulture on ancient societies.

11. *A History of West Africa,* by Basil Davidson (Garden City, NY: Doubleday, 1966). A fine source of material on sub-Saharan societies prior to the colonial period. Davidson was for many years the leading authority on the subject.

In addition, there are informative chapters in the following books:

12. *Profiles in Ethnology,* by Elman Service (NY: Harper & Row, 1971). Short vignettes on a number of preliterate societies—many of them horticulturalists.

13. *Peoples of Africa,* by James Gibbs, ed. (NY: Holt, Rinehart, and Winston, 1965). An excellent collection of ethnographic reports on sub-Saharan peoples, most of whom are horticulturalists.

14. *Power and Privilege,* by Gerhard Lenski (NY: McGraw-Hill, 1984). Chapters 6 and 7 provide a more detailed discussion of inequality in horticultural societies than is possible in *Human Societies.*

QUIZ QUESTIONS

Fill-in-the-Blank

1. The first horticultural societies developed about _____ years ago in the area of the world known as the _____.

2. Three things have been identified as important causes of the shift to horticulture. They are (1) _____, (2) _____, and (3) _____.

3. The simplest form of horticulture is called _____ or _____ cultivation.

4. The best environment for such cultivation is _____.

5. In such a system of cultivation, when the productivity of the soil declines after a few years of cultivation, the simplest way to restore its fertility is to _____.

6. The first *advanced* horticultural societies appeared about _____.

7. One of the first metals used by (advanced) horticultural societies was _____.

8. Bronze is an alloy of two metals: _____ and _____.

9. An unusual feature of the kinship systems of horticultural societies is the relatively high incidence of _____ kinship.

10. Horticultural societies are also distinguished by the high incidence of religions based on _____.

11. Some people have argued that technological *advance* can be accompanied by moral *regression.* List some of the things that are more common in horticultural than in hunting and gathering societies that would support such an argument.

    (1) _____ (2) _____ (3) _____
    (4) _____ (5) _____

12. The adoption of horticulture made a number of social changes (e.g., urbanization, increased division of labor, and the political state) possible because it had the potential to produce a stable _____ .

13. Approximately what percentage of advanced horticultural societies practice some form of slavery? _____

14. A racist or racialist theory is one that asserts that differences in sociocultural development are the result of differences in _____ .

True or False

15. Cultivation in horticultural society was more likely to be the major responsibility of women than of men.

16. The technology of making pottery probably contributed to the development of metallurgy.

17. In horticultural societies, the ashes of burned trees and bushes must be swept from fields before they can be cultivated.

18. Head-hunting and ceremonial cannibalism are more likely to be found in horticultural societies than they were in hunting and gathering societies.

19. Bronze was the first metal used by horticulturalists.

20. Comparisons of the development of cultivation in China and the Middle East support *unilinear* theories of evolution.

21. Advanced horticultural societies had an average population of about 5,000 people.

22. Horticultural societies had homicide rates that were much lower than those found in recent years in the United States.

23. The "cult of the warrior" may have produced an increase in female infanticide.

24. Horticulture, for the first time, made the conquest and control of people profitable, and metal weapons helped make it possible.

25. Extended kin groups are also sometimes called clans.

26. Once horticulture developed, a stable economic surplus followed automatically.

27. A society in which political and religious activities are closely tied together is called a "theocracy."

Multiple Choice

28. Which of the following has been identified as *one of the most important* causes of the shift to horticulture?

a) population growth
b) increasing human intelligence
c) dissatisfaction with a nomadic lifestyle
d) the desire for progress and human betterment
e) none of the above

29. The shift from hunting and gathering to horticulture was:
    a) rapid
    b) gradual
    c) of little importance in the long run
    d) all of the above
    e) none of the above

30. Walled cities are evidence of the increase in _____ that followed the adoption of horticulture.
    a) matrilineal kinship
    b) warfare
    c) environmental instability
    d) the division of labor
    e) trade and commerce

31. In slash-and-burn horticulture, when soil fertility declines, the land is:
    a) plowed under
    b) reignited and allowed to burn again
    c) abandoned until the trees grow back
    d) sold
    e) used as a ceremonial burial center

32. Which of the following contributed to the development of metallurgy in horticultural societies?
    a) a sedentary lifestyle
    b) an increase in the use of clay containers
    c) the invention of kilns
    d) all of the above
    e) none of the above

33. Which of the following has the highest rate of homicide?
    a) the United States
    b) the most violent cities in the United States
    c) simple hunting and gathering societies
    d) advanced hunting and gathering societies
    e) horticultural societies

34. Which type of society has the *highest* incidence of slavery?
    a) hunting and gathering
    b) simple horticultural
    c) advanced horticultural
    d) agrarian
    e) industrial

35. Which of the following is *not* more common in horticultural than in hunting and ga-
    thering societies?
    a) warfare
    b) ceremonial cannibalism
    c) matrilineal kinship
    d) nomadism
    e) the requirement of a bride price

36. Horticultural societies in the New World are especially important for ecological--
    evolutionary theory, because they:
    a) provide an independent test of its basic tenets
    b) did not develop elaborate political systems
    c) were not as violent or warlike as were other horticulturalists
    d) did not have elaborate religious systems
    e) all of the above

37. Which of the following is a consequence of a stable economic surplus?
    a) an increased division of labor
    b) urban communities
    c) multicommunity societies
    d) formation of states
    e) all of the above

38. The incidence of matrilineal kinship is *greater:*
    a) the greater the contribution of women to subsistence
    b) the higher the geographic latitude
    c) the greater the reliance on hunting and herding
    d) the lower the geographic latitude
    e) none of the above

39. Perhaps the most compelling argument against racist or racialist theories is the fact
    that the technologically most advanced societies in one era:
    a) are in different regions of the world than the most advanced societies in other eras
    b) are inhabited by people of a "race" different from that of the most advanced
       societies of other eras
    c) are not the most advanced societies in previous and following eras
    d) all of the above
    e) none of the above

40. Which of the following is/are typical of horticultural societies?
    a) ancestor worship
    b) warfare
    c) slavery
    d) all of the above
    e) none of the above

Essay/Study Questions

41. Why is it now generally believed that hunters and gatherers were *reluctant* to adopt
    horticulture? What processes ultimately forced them to do it?

42. What is an "economic surplus"? Was it an *automatic* consequence of plant cultivation? What important social changes followed the production of economic surpluses?

43. What factors help to explain the dramatic increases in warfare that occurred in *advanced* horticultural societies?

44. Why was metallurgy such an important innovation? What role did pottery play in its development? Could hunting and gathering societies have developed metallurgy?

45. How were kinship and politics intertwined in horticultural societies? Why would a ruler fear his brothers and uncles?

46. Why was slavery so rare in hunting and gathering societies, and so common in advanced horticultural?

47. What do the large religious structures and monuments constructed in advanced horticultural societies tell us about the economies, the political systems, the social structures, and the religious beliefs of these societies?

NOTES

---

[1] It is important to remember that the shift to horticultural was gradual, and many of its effects were slow to develop. Moreover, as many of the statistics in Chapter 6 show, simple horticultural societies were not very different from hunting and gathering societies, but advanced horticultural societies were *quite* different.

[2] We have to be careful not to *assume* that since *we* are sedentary, hunters and gatherers *wanted to be* sedentary and would "jump at the chance" to be so. The evidence indicates that they probably resisted settling down, and some of the problems associated with a sedentary lifestyle make this resistance understandable.

[3] "Swidden" is an Old English word meaning "burned clearing."

[4] I saw one comparison that indicated that in slash-and-burn horticulture there are 16 calories of food-energy produced for every 1 calorie of energy expended to produce it (a 16:1 return ratio), whereas in mechanized agriculture only 3 food-energy calories are produced for every calorie expended to produce it (a 3:1 return ratio). Marvin Harris argues that if you also consider the calories of energy required to ship, process, package, store, and retail the food, there is actually a net loss. It takes more calories of energy to produce the food than are contained in the food that reaches the consumer (see "The Industrial Bubble" in *Cannibals and Kings* [NY: Random House, 1977]).

[5] This is the source of another one of those cross-societal-type misunderstandings. Since agriculture requires that cultivated fields be cleared of trees and stumps, and horticulture requires that trees be allowed to return before cultivation, a forest has a different "meaning" in each system of cultivation. To a horticulturalist, uncultivated forest is an integral part of the cycle of cultivation; to the agriculturalist, it is abandoned and unused land. Thus, agriculturalists would sometimes seize "unused" forest/frontier and put it under cultivation. To the horticulturalists, this was theft; to the agriculturalists, it was merely putting unused forest/frontier to productive use.

[6] In the chapters "Pig Lovers and Pig Haters" and "Primitive War" in *Cows, Pigs, Wars, and Witches* (NY: Random House, 1974), Marvin Harris describes the effects of population growth on horticulture, and how warfare may have indirectly reduced rates of population growth in some horticultural societies.

[7] These figures are obtained by adding the percentage of societies where warfare is "perpetual" to the percentage in which it is "common" (e.g., 0 + 27 for hunting and gathering societies).

[8] Bruce Knauft's article, "Reconsidering Violence in Simple Societies," was in *Current Anthropology*, August–October 1987, Volume 28, pages 457–500.

[9] See pages 55–56 of this *Primer and Guide*.

[10] Further technological "advances" generally reduced the profitability and viability of slavery; the probability of slavery declines with the advent of agriculture and becomes virtually zero in industrial societies.

[11] As we noted in Chapter 5, infanticide was an unpleasant fact of life in hunting and gathering societies. If a woman with a small child gave birth to another, the newborn was often abandoned or killed, especially if caring for it would endanger the life of the child she already had. It was generally not sex-specific, however (i.e., it made little or no difference what the sex of the newborn was). To the extent that warfare (and perhaps the decreased productivity of hunting) increased the "value" of males, female infants were more likely to be killed or abandoned than were males. Warfare also greatly affected the social standing of women in general (see "The Savage Male" in Marvin Harris, *Cows, Pigs, Wars, and Witches* [NY: Random House, 1974]).

[12] Since these are *horticultural societies* (i.e., horticulture produces *most* of the subsistence) and hunting and herding are predominantly male activities, the lower the contribution of hunting and herding to total subsistence (e.g., 15 percent or less), the greater the contribution of females (and *vice versa*). Matrilineal kinship is found in 30 percent of the societies where female contributions to subsistence are greater, and 14 percent where they are less.

[13] The estimate of the amount of time required for biological change is based on the assumption that a generation of humans is 25 years (clearly a *minimum* figure) and the argument that it is only after 1,000 to 10,000 generations of a population are subjected to selective pressures that the population will evidence significant biological change (e.g., speciation).

7

Agrarian Societies

CHAPTER SUMMARY

This chapter begins with a discussion of the problems of cultivation that pushed societies to adopt the plow, and then explores the effects of the shift from hoe horticulture to plow agriculture on the structure of societies and social life. It examines agrarian societies from the time of their emergence in the Middle East around 3000 B.C. to the beginning of the modern industrial era. Once again, it focuses on the changes that occurred in all of their major institutional systems, giving special attention to the consequences of the growth of the economic surplus: further growth in the size and complexity of social organization, development of political and military "bureaucracies," emergence of monetary systems and growth in trade, increased specialization within and between societies, emergence of universal faiths, and very divergent prospects and lifestyles of the richest, most privileged, and the poorest, least privileged, members of agrarian societies. Late in the chapter, there is a discussion of *variations* among agrarian societies, including a brief examination of *frontier* societies, which have a special relevance for American, Australian, and Canadian histories. The chapter ends with a model (Figure 7.6, page 175) that summarizes the changes that occurred as a result of the adoption of this new mode of subsistence.

Evidence of the first agrarian societies—societies that depended on the cultivation of fields with plows for most of their food—comes from about 3000 B.C., or about 5,000 years ago.[1] Again, this pathbreaking technological development occurred in the Middle East. In some ways the plow was simply an extension of earlier efforts to maintain soil fertility in the face of increasing population and a growing demand for food (e.g., the hoe, fertilizer), but it was an extension that had *profound* consequences.

In fact, it is not an exaggeration to say that the plow was the technological foundation of what we have come to call "civilization." Rather than cultivating small garden plots for a few years, a farmer now could, with proper irrigation and fertilization, keep large *fields* under *continuous* cultivation. Thus, use of the plow and the harnessing of animals to pull it dramatically increased the *potential* productivity of farmers and of the land they cultivated (see illustration on page 138).

Actualization of this potential would not only enable societies to support much larger populations, but it would also greatly increase the size of the *economic surplus* that could be produced. Thus, it could greatly exaggerate and extend many of the developments that followed the initial adoption of plant cultivation (horticulture)—growth in the *scale* of societies (i.e., increased population *and* areal expanse), development of professional armies, an increase in the number and scale of wars of conquest, development of more powerful and more centralized governments, greater occupational specialization, increased regional trade and commerce, and more extensive social inequality.

To better grasp the magnitude of this increase in scale, consider the following facts. The largest simple agrarian society, Egypt, with a population of 15 million, was three times the size of the *largest* horticultural society. Yet, the largest advanced agrarian societies had populations in the hundreds of millions and thus were more than *ten times* the size of Egypt. Incredibly, the largest advanced agrarian society—mid-nineteenth-century China, with its population of about 400 million—was *10 million times the average size of hunting and gathering societies!*

The areal expanses of agrarian societies and empires also greatly exceeded those of previous societies. To get a better sense of how much larger they were, consider the fact that the Incan empire, one of the largest horticultural empires, covered an area of 350,000 square miles—no mean achievement, given the limits of available communications and transportation technologies. Nonetheless, agrarian empires often covered ten to twenty times that area. For instance, the Roman Empire covered 2 million square miles; China has been as large as 4 million square miles; and Russia under Peter the Great comprised nearly 6 million square miles of territory.

Not surprisingly, these increases in the *scale* of societies created unprecedented problems of organization. Never before had societies confronted the problem of organizing so many people distributed over such large territories. Furthermore, since empires typically expanded through conquest, they faced the additional problems of administering and organizing previously autonomous populations who spoke different languages, followed different customs, and practiced different religions.

As a result, new systems of organization emerged. Kinship still played an important role in *individuals'* lives—as it continues to do today—and it provided the nucleus of the organization of the ruling elite, but it was incapable of structuring all or most of the social relations among the populations of agrarian societies. The reasons are simple. First, kinship becomes quite cumbersome in a large population. Since kinship systems require one to know his/her *specific* relationship to another before s/he knows how to relate to them, in a large population a good deal of time would be consumed tracing one's heritage to locate a common ancestor. And, if two individuals could not locate a common ancestor, *they would have no basis for relating to one another;* it is impossible for kinship to organize and structure relationships among people who have no recognizable biological ties to one another.

One important organizational invention of this era, which has now become quite familiar to us, is "bureaucracy."[2] Bureaucratic organization is distinguished by its highly developed division of labor, in which specialized tasks are assigned to "experts," and by its hierarchy of authority, which coordinates the efforts of these specialists (e.g., see Figure 7.2 on page 143). In contrast to kinship, which organizes relationships among *individuals,* bureaucracies organize relationships among *positions.*[3] Thus, the coming and going of individuals is not as disruptive in bureaucratic organizations as it is in systems based on kinship. As long as *positions* are filled by people with the requisite skills, the organization can continue to operate. Thus, over the long term, bureaucratically organized armies and political administrations were less susceptible to disruption and disorganization than were systems based on kinship. They were thus more likely to be successful and to survive.

The increased inequality that developed in most agrarian societies also had important organizational consequences.[4] Not only did the polarization of strata slow down the rate of innovation—the *incentive* for innovation was separated from the *knowledge* that made innovation possible—but it also created a special "dynamic" in these societies (see Figure 7.3 on page 147 and Figure 7.6 on page 175). Since elites did not have effective mechanisms for *significantly increasing the production of peasants already under their control,* the primary means available to them for increasing their wealth was to *increase the amount of land and the number of peasants they controlled.* Thus, the surplus extracted from peasants and serfs was often put to the task of acquiring control over more land and more peasants.

A powerful tool in this quest was the professional army. Although most were small by modern standards—often numbering only in the hundreds or thousands—they were a formidable force at the time. Peasants and peasant militias were no match for well-equipped, well-trained *armies* of full-time soldiers. Thus, agrarian technology, professional armies, and wars of conquest touched off a "positive feedback" cycle that gave rise to one of the distinctive features of this era—the cyclical rise and fall of empires.

Large military machines fueled by the booty of conquest could expand the boundaries of empires—conquering more territory increased the size of the surplus, and this greater surplus could finance a larger army, which, in turn, could conquer more territory—but the military *reach* of these systems easily exceeded their political and economic *grasp*. It was easier to *conquer* than it was to *control* people and territory. In part this was a problem posed by the limited technologies of communication and transportation, but it was also a result of the limits imposed by existing systems and methods of organization. The problems of integration and control in empires gave rise to a number of institutional innovations.

One of the mechanisms used to extend control over previously autonomous communities was the imposition of a single, standardized set of laws over the entire territory of the empire. To the degree this was accomplished, local elites could be replaced by, or subordinated to, the central political elites of empires. It is no accident, therefore, that historically important, standardized systems of law bear the names of military conquerors (e.g., Hammurabi, see http://www.wsu.edu/~dee/meso/code.htm; Napoleon, see http://www.napoleon-series.org/research/government/c_code.html).

The extension of political and legal control over diverse communities and peoples also gave rise to a revolutionary change in religious beliefs and religious organization. *Universal* faiths—those that believers feel should be adopted by, and spread to, all people—develop for the first time in these societies (see pages 164–66). Prior to the development of multi-community societies and extensive empires, religion was generally regarded as the *private* concern of households, local groups, and communities. It was not something that people felt should be shared with others, especially not with strangers. As we are now well aware, this is not the case with Islam, Christianity, and Buddhism.

The increased surplus produced and extracted from a growing number of peasants in agrarian societies also meant that a large number of other people were freed from the need to produce their own food and fibers. As a result, the first true cities—places where large concentrations of people *resided*—emerged. Very few people resided in the "cities" of horticultural societies. In fact, they are more accurately described as ceremonial centers than as urban communities. Large numbers of people assembled in these places only temporarily, for important religious and political ceremonies; they did not live there.

The cities of agrarian societies, although small by modern standards with populations typically only in the tens of thousands, were places of stark contrast. The "surplus" peasant sons and daughters who migrated to the cities in search of a livelihood often ended up as beggars, thieves, and prostitutes. Against this backdrop of human misery and "expendables," however, could be seen the richest and most powerful members of the society with their retinue of slaves, servants, and retainers. There were relatively few people between these extremes. What we now consider the "middle classes"—merchants, artisans, clerks (scribes), etc.—were much smaller proportions of the population of typical agrarian societies than they are of industrial societies. Figure 7.5 (page 171) shows that their economic position was also generally lower than that which we associate with contemporary occupants of these professions.

Moreover, in an ironic and macabre twist of fate, the bargaining position and economic well-being of non-elites was often improved by epidemic diseases and the high mortality rates found in agrarian cities. As is true of other commodities, the value of labor and peasants was related to their supply. When there was a "surplus" of these commodities, their value was low. The fact that cities were such unhealthy and dangerous places (e.g., see pages 150–152) meant that avenues of upward mobility did exist. In fact, in the face of their high mortality rates, the only way cities could maintain their populations was through a constant influx of people from rural areas. Furthermore, the concentration of populations in cities and the increase in inter-societal trade also provided ideal conditions for the development and spread of a number of new diseases (e.g., bubonic plague), which, by drastically reducing their numbers, periodically raised the value and bargaining position of peasants and other non-elites.[5]

It is also ironic that the development of systems of writing and calculating—some of the greatest achievements of "civilization"—were probably not motivated by the needs of artistic expression, philosophy, or science, but by the much more mundane needs of tax assessors, tax collectors, merchants, and the ruling political and religious elites. Record keeping was a serious problem in such large and complex societies. Who owned what land? How much tax did they owe? Who had paid their taxes? How many workers could a village supply for public works such as irrigation systems or religious monuments? Systems of writing, calculating, and measuring were spurred on by these problems, and the surplus extracted by centralized elites freed increasing numbers of people to develop and employ them.

Trade also increased among these societies as a result of the large economic "surplus" extracted by elites. In fact, a "positive feedback" cycle often developed between trade and "money" in these societies and empires. Trade *possibilities* within and between societies increased with a growing surplus, but as long as *barter* was the dominant method of exchange, trade was severely limited. This tension between the increasing trade *potential* and the existing economic *barriers* to trade created a strong pressure to develop a medium of exchange that would facilitate trade. To be effective, such a medium should be easily divisible, durable, and trustworthy.

Given its divisibility and inherent value as food, grain provided an early currency.[6] Its major limitation was durability—it could not be stored indefinitely without spoiling or rotting. Once discovered, gold and silver were, and continue to be, useful in this regard because they are durable, have intrinsic value, and are finely divisible. Use of gold and silver made greater trade possible, and this, in turn, gave rise to further economic specialization, increased production, and a demand for *more* gold and silver. Their basic limitation as a currency was what helped give them their intrinsic value—their scarcity.[7]

Frontier agrarian societies are discussed just before the end of the chapter. These societies are distinguished for a number of reasons. First, they are an important part of the heritage of many contemporary industrial societies—for example, the United States, Canada, Australia, New Zealand. Second, they not only provide a model of variations on the basic agrarian theme, but they played an important role in making the Industrial Revolution *possible*. As we will see in Chapter 9, in addition to providing a massive influx of raw materials and absorbing "surplus" population at a time when agrarian Europe was in desperate need of both, they also provided arenas where innovation and individual effort were more directly tied to economic prosperity than they were in mature agrarian societies.

Figure 7.6 on page 175 summarizes some of the most important social innovations and changes that were spurred by the shift from horticulture to agriculture.

IMPORTANT TERMS

horti/agri-cultura	bureaucracy	millennia
hieroglyphic/hieratic	scribe	barter
money	expendables	frontier society
positive/negative feedback	empire	life expectancy
fertility/mortality	Black Plague	serf/peasant
command/market economies	guilds	universal faith
proprietary theory of the state		

RECOMMENDED READING

1. *Man Makes Himself,* by V. Gordon Childe (NY: Mentor, 1951). Chapters 7–9 provide a classic account of the rise of agrarian societies.

2. *Plough and Pasture,* by E. Cecil Curwen and Gudmund Hatt (NY: Collier Books, 1961). Good introduction to agricultural tools and techniques and their history—especially Part I, Chapters 4 and 5, and Part II, Chapters 16–18.

3. *Writing: The Story of Alphabets and Scripts,* by Georges Jean (NY: Henry N. Abrams, 1992), and *Numbers: The Universal Language,* by Denis Guedj (NY: Henry N. Abrams, Inc., 1997). Two beautifully illustrated and well-written paperbacks on the origins and development of these important symbol systems.

4. *The Merchant Class of Medieval London,* by Sylvia Thrupp (Ann Arbor, MI: University of Michigan Press, 1962). Excellent analysis of an interesting and important segment of agrarian societies.

5. *Lord and Peasant in Russia from the Ninth to the Nineteenth Century,* by Jerome Blum (Princeton, NJ: Princeton University Press, 1961). Outstanding case study of one agrarian society.

6. *Life on the English Manor: A Study of Peasant Conditions, 1150–1400,* by H.S. Bennett (London: Cambridge University Press, 1960). Another excellent case study.

7. *The Politics of Aristocratic Empires,* by John Kautsky (Chapel Hill, NC: University of North Carolina Press, 1982). Excellent discussion of the polities of agrarian societies. Among other things, it notes that violence in "traditional" agrarian societies (those with little commercial development) was almost exclusively horizontal—intraclass.

8. *A History of Technology,* by Charles Singer (Oxford: Clarendon, 1965). A good source of information on the technologies of agrarian societies.

9. *The Preindustrial City,* by Gideon Sjoberg (NY: Free Press, 1960). Comprehensive survey of the urban component of agrarian societies.

10. *Cortes and the Downfall of the Aztec Empire: A Study in a Conflict of Cultures,* by Jon Manchip White (NY: Carroll & Graf, 1989). White's discussion of Hernan Cor-

tes shows how the stratification system of agrarian societies and the practice of primogeniture provided a strong motivation for the younger sons of the aristocracy to risk life and limb in the quest to explore and conquer the New World.

11. *The Tribes of Yahweh,* by Norman Gottwald (Maryknoll, NY: Orbis, 1979); *Iceland: The First New Society,* by Richard Tomasson (Minneapolis, MN: University of Minnesota Press, 1980); and *The Cossacks,* by Philip Longworth (NY: Holt, Rinehart, and Winston, 1970). Three excellent case studies of frontier societies.

12. *Christ Stopped at Eboli,* by Carlo Levi (NY: Farrar, Straus, 1947); and *Bread and Wine,* by Ignazio Siloni (NY: New American Library, 1986). Two moving accounts of peasant life in Italy. Antidotes for those who romanticize the rural past.

13. *Plagues and Peoples,* by William McNeill (Garden City, NY: Anchor, 1976). An excellent discussion of the relationship between societal evolution and disease in general, and the black plague in particular.

14. *The Black Death,* by Robert Gottfried (NY: Free Press, 1983). Very good source on the social structure of Medieval Europe and the impact of the black plague on it.

15. *Power and Privilege,* by Gerhard Lenski (NY: McGraw-Hill, 1984). Detailed analysis of stratification in agrarian societies.

QUIZ QUESTIONS

Fill-in-the-Blank

1. Evidence indicates that the first agrarian societies developed about (when) _____ in the part of the world known as the (where) _____.

2. The plow helped to deal with two major problems confronting cultivators: _____ and _____.

3. A society in which religion and politics are tightly interwoven is called a _____.

4. Because virtually all economic decisions are made by and for political elites in agrarian societies, their economies are called _____.

5. Although agrarian societies had the first true cities, only about ____ percent of their populations lived in cities.

6. The practice of using the political state for the personal benefit of the *rulers* is known as the _____.

7. Three major *universal* faiths that developed in the agrarian era are: _____, _____, and _____.

8. Which was more responsible for differences among agrarian societies: differences in biophysical or social environments? _____

9. A branch or colony of an agrarian society established in a new territory outside the control of the central political elite is called a/an _____ society.

10. The largest horticultural society may have had a population of _____ million people, but the largest advanced agrarian society had a population of ____ million.

True or False

11. The rate of innovation in many agrarian societies was lower than one would expect, given their population sizes and large stores of cultural information.

12. The governing elites of most agrarian societies considered farming to be hard but rewarding and honorable work.

13. The elites of many agrarian societies considered peasants to be similar to livestock.

14. The rural areas of agrarian societies typically had higher rates of mortality than urban areas.

15. Statistics indicate that, on average, in agrarian societies people who reached adulthood generally died before their thirtieth birthday.

16. The ruling elite, which constituted 2 percent or less of the population, often claimed more than half of the total income of agrarian societies.

17. Buddhism is one of the universal faiths that developed in agrarian societies.

18. British settlements in the United States, Australia, and New Zealand were *frontier* societies.

19. In traditional agrarian empires, most social conflict was between the upper and the lower classes.

20. The increased volume of trade between societies contributed to the slowdown in the rate of innovation in agrarian societies.

Multiple Choice

21. The earliest evidence of the use of plows is found in:
    a) England (Europe)
    b) Australia (Oceania)
    c) Mexico (North America)
    d) Mesopotamia (Middle East)
    e) Peru (South America)

22. Which of the following is *not* a consequence of adoption of the plow?
    a) better control of weeds
    b) more effective maintenance of soil fertility
    c) harnessing of animal power

    d) permanent cultivation of fields

    e) declining social inequality

23. According to the text, the first living things that pulled plows were probably:
    a) humans
    b) goats
    c) horses
    d) mules
    e) llamas

24. Which of the following developed for the first time in agrarian societies?
    a) full-fledged cities
    b) government bureaucracies
    c) money
    d) professional armies
    e) all of the above

25. The most important stimulus to develop systems of writing and counting was probably:
    a) the need for artistic expression
    b) the need to record the results of scientific experiments
    c) the need to record important religious experiences
    d) the need to keep records of business transactions
    e) the need to collect and report the news

26. Which of the following is/are (an) important cleavage(s) in agrarian societies?
    a) the split between the governing class and the mass of peasants
    b) the split between the small literate minority and the large illiterate majority
    c) the split between the urban minority and the rural majority
    d) all of the above
    e) none of the above

27. What percentage of the population of advanced agrarian societies typically lived in cities?
    a) 5–10 percent
    b) 10–20 percent
    c) 20–30 percent
    d) 30–40 percent
    e) more than 40 percent

28. The largest agrarian societies had populations of:
    a) less than 10 million
    b) 10–50 million
    c) 50–100 million
    d) 100–400 million
    e) more than a billion

29. The birthrates of agrarian societies have been about _____ per 1,000 population.
    a) 20
    b) 40
    c) 60

    d) 80
    e) 100

30. According to Table 7.1 (p. 151), who died at an earlier age?
    a) men
    b) women

31. An economy in which economic decisions are made by political elites is:
    a) a command economy
    b) a political economy
    c) a market economy
    d) a capitalist economy
    e) a corporate economy

32. In agrarian societies, differences between the elite and the peasantry were so great that the peasantry were sometimes listed together with _____ by the elite.
    a) livestock
    b) obituaries
    c) criminals
    d) vagabonds
    e) aristocrats

33. According to the boxed insert, *Mother Goose* rhymes are an indicator of:
    a) how happy people were in agrarian societies
    b) the natural, healthy lifestyle of peasants in agrarian Europe
    c) how lazy most people were in agrarian societies
    d) the poverty and despair of many people in agrarian societies
    e) the literary creativity of its author

34. According to figures in Chapter 7 (page 159), which of the following is the *cheapest* method of transporting goods?
    a) pack mule
    b) pack donkey
    c) wheelbarrow
    d) railroad
    e) (human) carrying by pole

35. In agrarian societies, the governing class viewed government offices as:
    a) things that could be owned
    b) things to be used for private advantage and private gain
    c) things that could be bought and sold
    d) all of the above
    e) none of the above

36. Which of the following is most likely to be able to *remove* and *replace* the ruler of an advanced agrarian society?
    a) a relative of the ruler
    b) the peasants
    c) the artisans and merchants
    d) an expendable
    e) a serf

37. Politics in agrarian societies were:
    a) based on the will of the people
    b) often violent
    c) a duty that the elite reluctantly accepted
    d) more democratic than they are in modern industrial societies
    e) none of the above

38. The governing class of agrarian societies, which constituted about 2 percent of the total population, typically controlled about _____ percent of the total income.
    a) 10
    b) 25
    c) 50
    d) 75
    e) 90

39. Which of the following is *not* a universal faith discussed in Chapter 7?
    a) Buddhism
    b) Islam
    c) Animism
    d) Christianity
    e) none of the above (all of these are universal faiths discussed in Chapter 7)

40. Examples from the Roman Empire and agrarian Europe suggest that recreational activities in these societies could be:
    a) brutal and violent
    b) enjoyable and educational
    c) fun and games
    d) liberating and beneficial
    e) none of the above

41. Starting from the poorest and least powerful, and moving toward the richest and most powerful, in what order would you find the following economic (strata) classes in a "typical" advanced agrarian society?
    a) expendables, merchants, governing class, retainers and priests, ruler
    b) retainers and priests, merchants, expendables, governing class, ruler
    c) merchants, retainers and priests, expendables, governing class, ruler
    d) expendables, merchants, retainers and priests, governing class, ruler
    e) governing class, retainers and priests, expendables, merchants, ruler

42. The most important factor producing *differences* among agrarian societies is/are:
    a) differences in social environments
    b) differences in ideology
    c) differences in biophysical environments
    d) differences in religion
    e) none of the above

43. Which of the following is/are characteristic of *frontier* agrarian societies?
    a) an oversupply of labor
    b) a shortage of cultivatable land
    c) a very centralized and powerful government

    d) all of the above
    e) none of the above

44. One of the most important consequences of the growth of the economic surplus in
    agrarian societies was:
    a) the rise in the standard of living of the average member of society
    b) the decline in inequality
    c) the growth of the state and the power of the governing class
    d) all of the above
    e) none of the above

Essay/Study Questions

45. Early in the course, the claim was made that technological advance did not imply
    moral or ethical "progress." Considering the changes that occurred in societies since
    hunting and gathering, what evidence can you present to support or refute this claim?

46. How did the plow contribute to growth in inequality?

47. What was life like in a "typical" agrarian city? What kind of people lived and
    worked in them? Were they safe places to be? Why or why not?

48. What were politics and stratification like in advanced agrarian societies?

49. Why did empires develop and grow in the agrarian era? What effects did empire-
    building have on religion and the law?

50. Why did kinship cease to be the dominant principle of organization in agrarian socie-
    ties?

51. What is bureaucratic organization? Why did political and religious organizations
    become bureaucratic in the agrarian era?

52. Why do we have such a *romantic* image of life in agrarian societies? What facts
    about these societies challenge their idyllic image?

NOTES

[1] Ironically, although humans have spent more than 99 percent of their time on Earth in hunting and
gathering and horticultural societies, agrarian societies are more familiar to us. This is because we
know more about them from studying our own history, and because modern industrial societies still
reflect many aspects of their agrarian heritages. It is important to remember that the industrial era is
only about 200 years old. In fact, the United States was still basically an agrarian society—albeit a
"frontier" one—until nearly the end of the nineteenth century (about A.D. 1870).

[2] Technically, these early political administrations were not fully or completely "bureaucratic" in
the modern sense of the term, but key features of bureaucratic administration did develop in this
era.

[3] The former are sometimes referred to as "egocentric" and the latter "sociocentric" systems of
relationships. "Egocentric" systems center on, or revolve around, individuals; "sociocentric" sys-

tems center on, or revolve around, positions. In "egocentric" systems every individual (ego) confronts a *unique* web of relations (one's father is someone else's brother, cousin, uncle, etc.) and may be expected to act differently toward *each* of these relations. In contrast, sociocentric systems reduce the degree to which individuals have *unique* sets of relations and "standardize" the ways that individuals occupying different social positions relate to one another (e.g., customer/clerk, supervisor/subordinate).

[4] Figure 7.5 on page 171 depicts stratification in a "typical" agrarian society. Note that the vertical dimension of the figure indicates *ranking* of classes in terms of their power, privileges, and prestige, and the horizontal dimension indicates their relative or proportionate *sizes.*

[5] William McNeill's *Plagues and Peoples* (Garden City, NY: Anchor, 1976) is a fascinating account of the relationship between human populations and disease, with special attention to the causes and consequences of bubonic plague (also see *The Black Death,* by Robert Gottfried [NY: Free Press, 1983]).

[6] Modern societies use what is called a "fiat" currency. The value of this currency (e.g., our paper money) rests basically on a government *promise.* As a result, the value of the currency depends on how *believable* the promise is. In agrarian societies and empires, such promises had little credibility, and as a result such currencies had little value. What traders wanted was something that was *itself* valuable or useful.

[7] Figure 9.1 (page 194), shows how the massive increase in the supply of gold and silver that followed "discovery" of the New World disrupted the economic-political order of agrarian Europe and thereby helped pave the way for the Industrial Revolution.

8

Some Evolutionary Bypaths and a Brief Review

CHAPTER SUMMARY

This short chapter is divided into two parts. The first part briefly sketches the key features of three types of *environmentally specialized* societies—fishing societies, herding societies, and maritime societies—and discusses how they have influenced and been influenced by other societal types. The second part reviews trends and developments in the world system of societies from the hunting and gathering era to the eve of the Industrial Revolution. Figure 8.1 shows the trend in world population in relation to the emergence of horticulture, agriculture, and industrialization. It is argued that the historical record, to this point, provides substantial evidence in support of ecological-evolutionary theory (e.g., see Figure 3.4 on page 60).

The environmentally specialized societies distinguished in Chapter 4—fishing, herding, and maritime—are described and compared in this chapter. The brevity of the chapter is not an indication of the unimportance of these societal types, but rather a reflection of the unusual environments in which they have flourished and a recognition of the limits of what can be covered in a single textbook. In fact, even this brief discussion indicates a number of important ways in which they have impacted on, and affected, more "mainstream" societal types.

	Fish.	H&G	Herd.	S. Hort.
Median Community Size	90	40	72	138
Median Societal Size	90	40	5750	1500
Population/ Square Mile	10	0.6	02.1	13.8
% with Sedentary Communities	55	10	13	91
% Multicommunity Societies	13	15	68	51
% with Patrilineal Kinship	18	25	81	30
% with Slavery	51	11	82	15
% with Hereditary Slavery	30	2	61	5
% with Belief in a Creator God	9	4	73	10

The table on the previous page will facilitate comparisons among these environmentally specialized societies, and among them and some of the more typical societies at similar levels of general technological development.[1]

Fishing societies, the second oldest type of society we have distinguished, hunt on the seas and in streams rather than on the land. Such "hunting" is usually more productive, and it is also less likely (prior to industrialized fishing) to deplete the supply of animals that are hunted. This has generally produced somewhat larger, more sedentary communities and greater social inequality than is found in more "typical" hunting and gathering societies. Yet even they were usually absorbed or conquered when they came in sustained contact with more powerful horticultural or agrarian societies. Because they could not move and still retain their way of life, fishing societies became fishing *communities* in agricultural societies.

The levels of development attained by herding societies span the combined ranges of horticultural and agrarian societies. To keep their herds in good pasture, they are generally nomadic or seminomadic, and, although their communities are small—only about half as large as those of simple horticulturalists (72 versus 138)—their societies are quite large—more than three times the size of simple horticulturalists (5,750 versus 1,500). This disparity in the sizes of communities and societies clearly indicates that the majority (68 percent) of herding societies contain more than one community (i.e., they are multicommunity societies).

The mobility they attained by the harnessing and riding of domesticated animals enabled them to integrate previously autonomous societies, dispersed over a large geographical area, into a *single* society. It also contributed to making them formidable military powers. In fact, a number of herding societies conquered vast territories and built large empires (e.g., the Mongol, Mogul, and Ottoman empires). Ultimately, however, they were unable to hold these empires together and still retain their distinctive lifestyles, so many ended up either abandoning their pastoral life and being absorbed into agrarian societies or escaping to more marginal environments unsuited to cultivation (e.g., the arctic and desert) where they could continue herding.

Furthermore, because of the extensive material wealth they amassed, largely in the form of livestock, they were highly stratified and very patriarchal. In fact, they attained the dubious distinction of being the *most* likely of all the types of societies we have distinguished to have hereditary slavery. Indeed a majority (61 percent) of those for which we have evidence had this institution. They were also the most likely to have *patrilineal* kinship (82 percent). And, perhaps because of the model herding activities provided for them, they were the most likely to believe in a creator god who is concerned with, and actively supports, human morality (73 percent).[2]

Maritime societies are the rarest of all societal types (see the top of Figure 4.2 on page 67). Only a handful can be identified in history (e.g., the Phoenicians, Carthaginians, Venetians, Genoans, British), and today perhaps only one society—Singapore—can be considered a maritime society. This is because a maritime society is not simply a society with substantial overseas trade, but one that depends on such trade for *most* of its subsistence. The circumstances that would promote and sustain such a mode of subsistence are rare and often short-lived. Maritime societies could develop only *after* the emergence of societies with sustained surpluses that could be traded, and only *where* the seafaring technology and environment of a society enabled it to exploit this opportunity. Furthermore, once such a society developed, its existence was often threatened by the very societies with which it traded.

In addition to being rare, maritime societies are also unusual. Whereas (especially during the agrarian era) the agrarian societies with which they traded were typically monarchies or politically centralized empires dominated by land-owning and military elites that looked upon trade and commerce with contempt, maritime societies were typically (oligarchical) republics in which merchants and traders constituted the dominant class. They were thus unusually democratic, and because they were more favorably disposed toward commerce and trade, they were unusually innovative and productive.

Finally, to prepare the groundwork for a better understanding of the Industrial Revolution, the focus of Chapter 9, the chapter ends with a brief review of the developments that occurred from the first emergence of truly modern humans through the end of the agrarian era (about A.D. 1800). Some of the key trends and changes noted are:

Total human population increased by nearly 10,000 percent from the end of the hunting-gathering era to the end of the agrarian era! It went from some 10 million in 8000 B.C. to nearly a billion in A.D. 1800

Societies became larger, were more likely to be sedentary, were socially and technologically more complex, and were much more stratified.

The store of technological information increased greatly, in part because of inventions that facilitated the storage and processing of information—for example, writing, numerical systems, and so on—and improved communication—for example, movable type, improved transportation, and so on.

The rate of technological innovation also accelerated—with temporary exceptions—in *each* of the eras following that of hunting and gathering.

The growth in differences *within* societies was also accompanied by a growth in differences *among* societies. Whereas during the hunting and gathering era societies were fairly similar, by the end of the agrarian era societies differed greatly in such fundamental things as their size, technological power, and the form of their governments. They also occupied a wide variety of environments.

IMPORTANT TERMS

fishing	herding	maritime
New World	Old World	pastoral
(democratic) republic	oligarchy	monarchy
patriarchal	misnomer	bride price/bride service

RECOMMENDED READING

1. *Cultures of the North Pacific Coast,* by Philip Drucker (San Francisco, CA: Chandler, 1965). Beautifully illustrated and authoritative account of the fishing societies of the northwest coast (the Kwakiutl and others with their practice of the potlatch). When read along with comparable works on hunting and gathering societies, this book nicely illustrates the greater developmental possibilities inherent in a fishing technology.

2. "Pastoralism," by Lawrence Krader, in the *International Encyclopedia of the Social Sciences,* vol. 11, pp. 453–61. Good introduction to herding societies, with bibliography for further reading.

3. *The Rise of the West,* by W. H. McNeill (NY: Mentor, 1963). A look at Eurasia, showing the importance of herding peoples in shaping its history.

4. *The Royal Hordes: Nomad Peoples of the Steppes,* by E. D. Phillips (NY: McGraw-Hill, 1965). Interesting account of nomadic peoples up to the time of the Huns.

5. *The Phoenicians,* by Donald Harden (NY: Praeger, 1963). Good introduction to this important, but often neglected, set of maritime societies.

6. *Venice: A Maritime Republic,* by Frederic Lane (Baltimore, MD: Johns Hopkins, 1973). A comprehensive history of the rise and fall of Venice that centers on the influence of the sea and affairs nautical.

7. *Ships and Seamanship in the Ancient World,* by Lionel Casson (Princeton, NJ: Princeton University Press, 1971). A good history of seafaring, with many excellent illustrations.

QUIZ QUESTIONS

Fill-in-the-Blank

1. A society that derives most of its subsistence by "aquatic hunting" is called a/an _____ society.

2. A society that derives most of its subsistence by overseas trade is a/an _____ society.

3. A society with a pastoral economy is a/an _____ society.

4. At the end of the agrarian era, the population of the world was about _____ million.

True or False

5. Fishing societies are more likely to be sedentary than are hunting and gathering societies.

6. Herding societies are more likely to practice slavery than are fishing societies.

7. Fishing societies did not develop into more advanced types.

8. In the Old World, animals were domesticated about the same time that plants were domesticated.

9. Herding societies are the second oldest type of society.

10. Maritime societies are very likely to be patriarchal and to practice hereditary slavery.

Multiple Choice

11. Which environmentally specialized societies were *most* likely to be patriarchal and militaristic?
    a) fishing
    b) herding
    c) maritime

12. Which environmentally specialized societies were most likely to have a republican form of government?
    a) fishing
    b) herding
    c) maritime

13. Which type of society was most likely to be politically dominated by merchants and traders?
    a) fishing
    b) herding
    c) maritime
    d) hunting and gathering
    e) simple horticultural

14. Which type of society was most likely to have hereditary slavery?
    a) fishing
    b) herding
    c) maritime
    d) hunting and gathering
    e) simple horticultural

15. Which type of society had the highest population density?
    a) fishing
    b) herding
    c) maritime
    d) hunting and gathering
    e) simple horticultural

16. Which of the following societal types had larger communities?
    a) fishing
    b) herding

17. Which of the following societal types had larger populations?
    a) fishing
    b) herding

18. Which type of society is most likely to believe in a creator god?
    a) horticultural
    b) herding
    c) maritime
    d) fishing
    e) hunting and gathering

19. The rate of technological innovation generally _____ in each era following the hunting and gathering era.
    a) declined
    b) changed randomly
    c) went up and down
    d) accelerated
    e) remained unchanged

20. Inequality within societies generally _____ between the end of the hunting and gathering era, and the end of the agrarian era.
    a) increased
    b) declined
    c) remained the same

Essay/Study Questions

21. Why is it something of a "misnomer" to call any society a *fishing* society?

22. What is the origin of the word "nomad"?

23. What are some of the important contributions/innovations that environmentally specialized societies have made to other types of societies?

24. How do you explain the fact that herding *communities* are small, but herding *societies* are large?

25. In what ways are fishing societies *similar* to hunting and gathering societies? In what ways are they *different*?

26. How and why were the politics of maritime societies *unusual*?

27. Why did herding societies often end up being absorbed into agrarian societies they had previously "conquered"?

28. Why didn't fishing societies develop into more advanced types?

29. Describe the major differences in stratification in the environmentally specialized societies. What might account for these differences?

30. What was the world system of societies like at the end of the agrarian era? How had it changed since the hunting and gathering era?

NOTES

[1] Due to their rarity, no figures are calculated or presented for maritime societies.

[2] See Figure 4.4 on page 72 of *Human Societies* for a comparison with other societal types. The likelihood of such a belief in *agrarian societies* also increases with greater reliance on herding as a

supplement to subsistence. For instance, such beliefs are found in only 33 percent of agrarian societies in which herding contributes 6 to 15 percent of subsistence, but in more than 80 percent of those that rely on herding for 26 percent or more of their subsistence.

9

The Industrial Revolution

CHAPTER SUMMARY

This chapter examines the social and cultural revolution that produced the societies most familiar to us. It begins by analyzing the developments that led to the initial increase in the rate of technological innovation (Figure 9.1), moves on to a brief history of the four phases of the Industrial Revolution that have occurred thus far, and then considers the features of industrial societies that keep their rate of innovation high. Following this is a discussion of the varying levels of industrialization in contemporary societies (Table 9.3), and a map (Figure 9.2) of where industrial societies are in the world today. The final section of the chapter reviews the consequences of the Industrial Revolution, focusing primarily on the *initial* consequences while briefly summarizing the long-term consequences, which will be elaborated on in Chapters 10–13.

Although it began more than 200 years ago, the effects of the Industrial Revolution continue to be felt today. In fact, it is difficult to think of an aspect of human life that has not been transformed by it. Probably nothing other than the domestication of plants and animals has had such a profound effect on human societies and human life.

A number of developments and events contributed to the making of this revolution—increasing technological information, advances in transportation and communication, improvements in agriculture and animal husbandry—but nothing was more important than the European "discovery" and conquest of the New World (see Figure 9.1 on page 194 for a summary of some of the important causes and relationships). *In fact, it is probably not an exaggeration to say that without the conquest of this vast, sparsely settled land with its abundant natural resources, the Industrial Revolution would not have occurred.* It certainly was not inevitable.

The abundant raw materials in the New World helped fuel industrialization in Western Europe (which had used up much of its forests and was in need of more pasture and cultivatable land); the new territory enabled the productive settlement of the increasing numbers of "surplus" population generated by enclosure movements and improvements in agricultural technology. The large quantities of gold and silver that found their way into Europe from the New World increased the supply of "cash," which helped stimulate commerce and triggered spiraling inflation. Cash made the costs and returns of economic exchanges easier to calculate, and rising inflation made "traditional" economic pursuits increasingly unprofitable. As a result, many economic elites shifted their resources into more lucrative activities. Those that didn't were progressively weakened financially and politically. Thus, many of the features of feudal agrarian societies that were resistant to change and innovation were weakened or swept away.

The Industrial Revolution began when new (nonliving) sources of energy—for example, coal, petroleum, natural gas—were harnessed by machines and used to do work. For convenience, its onset is dated in the mid-eighteenth century (A.D. 1760) when the

93

first practical applications of steam power were achieved. It continues, at an accelerated pace, today. The details of the inventions and discoveries, although fascinating in their own right, are less important for our purposes than are the general trends of development and their social consequences. Therefore, when you read through the text discussion of its four phases, focus on the basic *themes* rather than on the names and dates of specific inventions/innovations. Pay particular attention to how innovations in one aspect of technology or the economy often spur changes and innovations in others. Productivity and innovation accelerated largely because when one "bottleneck" was overcome, this became an impetus for change in others.

The **first phase,** "Steam Engines, Iron, Coal, Textile Machines, Factories," of the Industrial Revolution (about 1760–1850) centered on machines that increased the productivity of human labor and machines that harnessed new sources of energy. In this phase the productivity of the textile, iron, coal, and machine-tool industries increased dramatically. It was also in this era that the *factory system* developed. It was a new way of organizing the labor of humans to accommodate the needs of machines and markets.[1]

The **second phase,** "Railroads, Steamships, Steel, Rubber, Farm Machines," (about 1850–1900) was marked by a number of improvements in transportation technologies—steamships, locomotives—that not only increased the demand for such things as coal and iron, but also helped supply these materials to a wider area by making it easier and cheaper to transport them (see the comparison of transportation costs on page 159). In the process, it tied societies and economies ever more closely together into a single global economic system. New systems of organization—for example, the multidivisional enterprise and corporation—also emerged and developed in this period.

The **third phase,** "Automobiles, Airplanes, Telephones, Electricity, Petroleum, Radios, Movies," (1900–1950) is marked by the development and spread of new technologies in the fields of transportation, communication, synthetic materials (e.g., plastics), the expansion of methods of harnessing and distributing energy, and the development of fearsome nuclear and biological weapons. It is characterized by tremendous growth in the production of automobiles, aircraft, telephones, and electricity.

The **fourth phase,** "Television, Computers, Transistors, The Internet, Plastics, Globalization,"—"the information age (1950–present)—is characterized by the expansion of television, computers, computer miniaturization, and the globalization of production.

The Industrial Revolution continues today in part as a result of the institutionalization of innovation in publicly funded institutions of science and in the research and development departments of private corporations. But it also continues because of the seemingly inexhaustible appetite industrial societies have for materials and energy (see pages 216–218 in Chapter 10 for some staggering statistics on the volumes of energy and materials produced and consumed annually in an industrial society). It has also been prodded periodically by the threat, occurrence, and ever-escalating technologies of war.

The total value of all goods and services produced by an economy (its GDP or Gross Domestic Product) is a good measure of the productivity of a society's technology, and thus it can be used as a measure of industrialization, especially after the size of the population producing it has been taken into account. Thus, *per capita* GDP will be used as a rough indicator of the degree to which a society is "industrialized" (see Table 9.3 on page 209). A list of advanced industrialized societies, which are the focus of Chapters 10 through 13, can be found on page 216 in Chapter 10, and a map (Figure 9.2) showing the location of industrial societies is on page 210.

Table 9.2 (page 204) shows the relative sizes of the largest national economies in the world today. Notice that the size of a nation's economy and its corresponding world influence is a *joint product* of its level of technological development *and* its population size. The reason that the United States, Japan, and Germany are such dominant members of the world economy—accounting for about 30, 13, and 5 percent of the Gross World Product, respectively—is that in addition to being highly advanced technologically, they are also *unusually large* for industrial societies. As we saw in Chapter 4, the median size of industrial societies today is about 10 million (see Table 4.2 on page 70). Yet the populations of the United States, Japan, and Germany are about 301, 127, and 82 million, respectively. As a result, their levels of economic production and the size of their markets dominate the world economy.[2]

It is important to recognize that the initial consequences of the Industrial Revolution were pretty grim—large numbers of people were uprooted and pushed into urban areas where rates of crime, vice, alcoholism, epidemic disease, poverty, and mental illness soared. Sanitation was poor, the work day was long (12–18 hours), pay was low, discipline in the workplace was punitive, and child labor was common (e.g., see the boxed insert, "Children and the Factory System," on page 212).[3]

The chapter closes with a brief discussion of the long-run consequences of the Industrial Revolution. Although not all of these are positive changes, they are markedly different from the short-term consequences, which were almost uniformly miserable. These long-run consequences will be discussed and explored in more detail in Chapters 10–13.

IMPORTANT TERMS

Gross Domestic Product	inflation	negative feedback
Gross World Product	factory system	positive feedback
Protestant Reformation	neophilic	per capita
multidivisional enterprise	corporation	

RECOMMENDED READING

1. *The Discoverers,* by Daniel Boorstin (NY: Random House, 1983). Details the developments and events leading up to European "discovery" of the New World. He also offers explanations of why the Chinese or Arabs did not make the "discovery," and effectively explodes the myth that Columbus was a "genius."

2. *Writing: The Story of Alphabets and Scripts,* by Georges Jean (NY: Henry N. Abrams, 1992). A beautifully illustrated and well-written account of the origins and development of written symbol systems and printing.

3. *The Town Labourer, 1760–1830,* by John and Barbara Hammond (London: Guild, 1949). Offers a vivid account of the impact of the Industrial Revolution on the lives of the new urban working class, drawn from contemporary sources.

4. *The Factory System,* by J. T. Ward, ed. (NY: Barnes and Noble, 1970). Provides material on the immediate consequences of the Industrial Revolution. It includes eyewitness accounts of workers testifying before Parliamentary committees (for an example of this kind of testimony, see the boxed insert, "Children and the Factory System," on page 212 of *Human Societies*).

5. *The Making of Economic Society,* by Robert Heilbroner (Englewood Cliffs, NJ: Prentice-Hall, 1975). Chapter 4 provides a good, short discussion of the Industrial Revolution.

6. "Epilogue: East and West in Retrospect," in *A History of Technology,* by Charles Singer (Oxford: Clarendon Press, 1965). Especially relevant to an understanding of the rise of the West, it provides badly needed historical and comparative perspective.

7. *Religion and the Rise of Capitalism,* by R. H. Tawney (New York: Mentor, 1947). An examination by a preeminent historian of the interplay between religion and the development of capitalism.

8. *The Visible Hand,* by Alfred D. Chandler, Jr. (Cambridge, MA: Belknap Press, 1977). Good review and discussion of the technological and organizational changes involved in the Industrial Revolution.

9. *Capital,* Volume 1, by Karl Marx (NY: International Publishers, 1967). Much of the sting of Marx's indictment of capitalism comes from his detailed discussion of the plight of the working class in newly industrialized societies. A good portion of his data comes from the various parliamentary investigations into the working and living conditions of the laboring classes in England.

10. *Historical Statistics of the United States: Colonial Times to 1970* and *Statistical Abstract of the United States,* by the U.S. Department of Commerce (http://www.census.gov); and the annual *World Development Report* and *World Development Indicators CD-ROM,* by the World Bank. Four good sources of basic economic and social data on contemporary and historical industrial societies.

QUIZ QUESTIONS

Fill-in-the-Blank

1. When the consequences of change produce more change, it is called _____ feedback.

2. The Industrial Revolution began (when) _____ (where) _____.

3. List some of the important factors that keep the Industrial Revolution going.

   (1) _____ (2) _____
   (3) _____ (4) _____
   (5) _____ (6) _____

4. Levels of industrialization in contemporary societies can be measured by _____.

5. Most industrial societies in the world today are found in _____ climates.

6. The harsh system of discipline and corporal punishment that workers were subject to following the Industrial Revolution is called the _____.

During what phase (1st, 2d, 3d, or 4th) of the Industrial Revolution:

7. were textiles at the forefront? _____

8. was aviation at the forefront? _____

9. was steam power applied to machines? _____

10. were nuclear *weapons* developed? _____

11. did the factory system develop? _____

12. were railroads at the forefront? _____

13. did petroleum *become* an important energy source? _____

14. were the first digital computers developed? _____

True or False

15. Barter is generally a more efficient method of organizing economic exchange than is money.

16. Although printing and movable type were invented in China, Gutenberg developed a system of printing with movable *letters*.

17. The Industrial Revolution started in 1760 and ended in 1830.

18. The first truly industrial society was Japan.

19. The textbook distinguishes four phases in the Industrial Revolution.

20. The multidivisional enterprise with salaried managers was an innovation developed in the first phase of the Industrial Revolution.

21. The first all-purpose electronic digital computer (ENIAC) was built about fifty years ago.

22. In the early stages of the Industrial Revolution, the living conditions of workers were already much better than those of the average peasant in an agrarian society.

23. Gasoline power was the first source of energy successfully applied to machines in the Industrial Revolution.

24. "Neophilia" is fear of new things.

25. One of the long-run consequences of industrialization has been a tripling of life expectancy.

Multiple Choice

26. Which of the following was *not* an important cause of the Industrial Revolution?
    a) advances in agriculture during the agrarian era
    b) discovery and conquest of the New World
    c) inflation
    d) an increase in the supply of gold and silver
    e) none of the above *(all* of these were important causes)

27. One of the ways Protestantism may have enhanced industrialization was by:
    a) increasing human kindness
    b) strengthening the bonds of nuclear families
    c) encouraging mass literacy
    d) advocating the rights of the poor
    e) protecting the environment

28. Which of the following was a consequence of discovery and conquest of the New World?
    a) an increase in European supplies of gold and silver
    b) new territories for settlement
    c) vast new supplies of raw materials
    d) increased world trade
    e) all of the above

29. Which of the following was *not* an important industry in the first phase of the Industrial Revolution?
    a) automobiles
    b) computers
    c) aviation
    d) nuclear power
    e) all of the above (*none* of these was an important industry then)

30. Which of the following was a new energy source first developed during the Industrial Revolution?
    a) wind
    b) falling water
    c) animals
    d) fire
    e) none of the above

31. Productivity increased during the Industrial Revolution primarily because of the development of:
    a) a healthier, stronger work force
    b) new machines and new energy sources
    c) larger populations
    d) improving climates
    e) none of the above

32. A good way to gauge *the degree* to which a contemporary society is industrialized is by considering:

   a) the proportion of its population employed in manufacturing
   b) the proportion of its population living in urban areas
   c) its per capita consumption of agricultural products
   d) its rate of violent crimes per capita
   e) its per capita gross domestic product

33. Which of the following is a factor that has kept the Industrial Revolution going?
   a) the rise of science
   b) the threat of war
   c) environmental feedback
   d) the desire for ever higher standards of living
   e) all of the above

34. Which of the following was a short-term consequence of the Industrial Revolution?
   a) improved sanitation
   b) better living conditions
   c) better health
   d) stronger family bonds
   e) none of the above

35. Which of the following is *not* a long-run consequence of the Industrial Revolution?
   a) a decline in the consumption of goods and services
   b) an increase in urban populations
   c) world population growth
   d) a more complex division of labor
   e) an increase in life expectancy

Essay/Study Questions

36. Sketch a model, in as much detail as you can, showing the most important causes of the Industrial Revolution and the interrelationships between them.

37. What roles did technological innovations in agriculture and printing play in producing the Industrial Revolution?

38. Why has the harnessing of inanimate (i.e., nonliving) forms of energy had such a dramatic impact on human societies and human life?

39. Give an example of how an innovation or breakthrough in one area of production/technology during the Industrial Revolution gave rise to changes in other areas.

40. What were some of the important consequences of "discovery" of the New World?

41. Would there have been an Industrial Revolution if the New World had *never* been discovered? What do you think would have happened if it had been discovered 1,000 years *earlier* (A.D. 500) or 1,000 years *later* (A.D. 2500)?

42. Are changing attitudes toward innovation in industrial societies better thought of as *causes* or *consequences* of the Industrial Revolution?

nOTES

[1] Notice that the *factory system* is not just a longer word for a factory, plant, or assembly line. It denotes a very strict hierarchical system of administration—modeled after a seventeenth or eighteenth century prison—in which discipline is harsh, and physical punishment and constraint are common (e.g., see the boxed insert, "Children and the Factory System," on page 212).

[2] As we will see in Chapter 14, this is one of the reasons that so much attention is now being directed to China. Given its immense population (about 1.3 *billion*), the opening of its markets and the development of its technology will have profound effects on the world economy. In fact, some economists predict that it will not be long before it surpasses Japan and the United States and becomes the world's *largest* economy!

[3] It is necessary to keep *these* conditions and those of peasants in agrarian societies in mind when evaluating the levels of, and trends in, living standards in advanced industrial societies.

10

Industrial Societies

Technologies and Economies

CHAPTER SUMMARY

The first of four chapters on modern industrial societies, Chapter 10 opens with the identification of twenty-nine industrialized societies. It then examines the technological foundation of industrial societies, the increasing productivity of labor, and the massive amounts of energy and materials that industrial societies produce and consume. This is followed by discussion of some of the key economic trends in industrial societies (increasing urbanization, rising productivity, increasing standards of living and per capita wealth, the shift toward more capital-intensive production) and changes in the labor force (the shift from primary industries, growth of white-collar jobs, increasing employment of women outside of households, growth in the size of work organizations, increasing occupational specialization, the formation of labor unions, and persistent problems with unemployment). Then attention is directed to the differences between command and market economies, and to how the inherent limitations and flaws in pure market economies have produced a trend toward mixed command-market economies in advanced industrial societies. The chapter closes with a discussion of the increasing interdependence of the economies of individual societies in the world system today.

It is only fitting that discussion of industrial societies begin with technology, because, according to ecological-evolutionary theory, changes in technology and in the amount of energy harnessed by it are what have made advanced industrial societies so different from their agrarian forebears.[1]

Table 10.1 (page 216) provides some key examples of the *magnitude* of this impact. For example, whereas it took 373 hours for a worker to produce 100 bushels of wheat in 1800, it took only 4 hours to produce that quantity of wheat in 1999. This is a reduction of 99 percent in the labor required! Similar reductions are shown for other agricultural products, and could be shown for a wide variety of nonfood products.

This reduction in *worker* hours, however, has been accomplished only by greatly increasing the energy and materials that are consumed in the production process. The magnitude of these increases is illustrated in the figures on pages 216–218. In fact, recent figures indicate that, *on a per capita basis,* industrial societies consume more than *four times* the energy consumed by contemporary (industrializing) agrarian societies, and more than *ten times* that consumed by contemporary (industrializing) horticultural societies. The United States, in fact, consumes the equivalent of *nine tons* of oil for every man, woman, and child in the society every year.

However, during previous periods of advances in subsistence technology, the population grew at a rate comparable to or faster than the rate of growth in productivity, and the average standard of living did *not* improve much. In contrast, population growth to-day has slowed sharply in industrial societies, and as a result, standards of living have greatly improved over what they were in agrarian and early industrial societies.[2] For ex-ample, in Great Britain and the United States, per capita GNPs are about thirteen times what they were in 1830 and 1870, respectively. These huge increases in the economic surpluses of industrial economies not only dramatically raised the average standard of living, but as we will see in Chapter 12, they have also generally reduced levels of ine-quality (e.g., see Table 12.2 on page 265).

Other notable trends in the economies of industrial societies are: (1) the urbanization of production; (2) the shift from labor-intensive to capital-intensive production; (3) the dra-matic decline in employment in primary (extractive) industries, modest increase in em-ployment in secondary (manufacturing) industries, and massive increase in employment in tertiary (service) industries; (4) increasing white-collar employment; (5) increasing em-ployment of women in the paid labor force (the causes and consequences of which we will discuss in more detail in Chapter 13); (6) growth in the size of work organizations; (7) an increase in occupational specialization (note some of the seemingly inane specialties listed on page 222); and (9) the development of labor unions.

Table 10.2 (page 221) shows the dramatic decline in primary industry employment and the massive increase in tertiary industry employment that occurred in the United States from 1840 to 2005. Notice that the decline in primary industry employment (from 69 percent to 2 percent) was *not* compensated for by increases in secondary industry em-ployment. In 1840 secondary industries employed 15 percent of the workforce, and they now employ about 19 percent, and even at their highest point they employed only about 30 percent of the working population. Tertiary industries have absorbed a much larger share of workers. Employment in them went from 16 percent to 79 percent, and the terti-ary sector continues to be the fastest growing employment sector in advanced industrial societies.[3] This change in occupational structure is also reflected in the disproportionate increase in white-collar employment. In 1900, 17 percent of the American workforce was employed in white-collar occupations; today 62 percent is (see Table 12.3 on page 268).[4]

These changes in the occupational structure have been responsible for a number of the fundamental social changes that have occurred in this period of U.S. history. We saw at the opening of the chapter that industrial technology has dramatically increased the productivity of agricultural labor. As this both "freed" and "pushed" agriculturalists off of farms, people migrated to cities in search of work.[5] Thus, the population of the United States shifted from being largely rural to being highly urbanized. Since many of the manufacturing centers were in the Northeast, this also meant there was a massive flow of people (many of whom were African American) from the rural South to the urban North. To the extent that the numbers of people exceeded or were ill-prepared for the opportunities that existed there, growing pockets of poverty grew, and conflict erupted periodically.

For a number of economic reasons, including the costs of energy and the costs of la-bor, in recent years there has been a large increase in the number of industries and firms locating in the South and the Southwest. As a result, for the first time in decades, there was a reversal in the South-to-North population flow.

As Table 10.3 (page 223) shows, labor unions have had very different histories in in-dustrial societies. In Scandinavian societies, more than 70 percent of the labor force is unionized and in recent years union membership has increased, whereas in Canada less than 30 percent, and in the United States only about 12 percent are, and union member-ship has declined.

Three broad types of economies can be distinguished in human societies— **subsistence, command,** and **market.** In subsistence economies, typical in hunting and gathering and simple horticultural societies, most families produce what they need and may trade in rarities and nonessentials. In agrarian command economies, which are layered on top of a subsistence (peasant) economy, elites control production and consumption (e.g., see Chapter 7, pages 153–161). In market economies, which are a relatively new innovation of industrial societies, goods and services are "freely" exchanged by their producers.

In the *ideal* market, price and corporate balance sheets drive *all* economic decisions, competition (or the potential for it) ensures that prices are set by supply and demand, and the government plays a very small role.[6] *Real* markets have rarely, if ever, attained this ideal. Furthermore, when they have come close to it, they have generally created such a negative public reaction that legislatures and governments have acted to draw them further away from this theoretical ideal.

First, public reaction to young children and women working long hours in dangerous jobs led to a number of laws restricting employment. Today most industrial societies have comprehensive bodies of law governing worker safety and compensation.[7] Laws restricting what can be bought and sold in markets, and regulating emissions (pollution) have also developed as problems with unrestrained production have become too obvious and too serious to ignore.[8] To the degree that such laws and regulations restrict economic behavior, markets are not free.

Second, as the name of the popular board game *Monopoly* suggests, if markets are allowed to operate without interference, *they self-destruct.* Table 10.4 (page 227) illustrates this process with hypothetical data. Larger companies (e.g., "Company A") with greater sales can sell their products more cheaply and thereby are in a position to put competitors out of business. If they do so, this further increases their sales and allows them to sell at even lower prices; if unchecked, this "positive feedback" system will ultimately result in a single company dominating the entire market. At this point competition ends, prices no longer reflect supply and demand, and a free market no longer exists. To prevent this, a variety of antitrust measures have been adopted in capitalist societies. Such legislation and government involvement mark a departure from the ideal of a free market.

A clear indication of this large and increasing involvement of government in market-oriented capitalist societies is the percentage of Gross Domestic Product *spent* by the governments of industrial societies shown in Table 10.6 (page 230). Although there is considerable variation in the level of spending among industrial societies—relatively high in most western European and Scandinavian societies, and low in the United States, Japan, and Australia—the governments of industrial societies, on average, now spend *more than five times* what they spent in 1870. In fact, despite its comparatively low level of spending, the United States today spends more than *nine times* what it did in 1870 (when it first crossed the industrial threshold).[9]

Nevertheless, Table 10.5 (page 229) clearly shows that despite the substantial and increasing government involvement in industrial economies and the legal barriers to *monopoly,* quite a few industries in the United States are *oligopolistic.*[10] As the text discussion indicates, although oligopolistic industries are more competitive than monopolistic ones, competition is likely to be less intense and less effective than it is in a competitive free market.

Taken together, all of this indicates that the economies of capitalist industrial societies are far from the idealized free markets advocated by Adam Smith (e.g., see Chapter 11, page 240–241), and as they continue to grow in size and influence, the governments of these societies are playing an increasing role. Thus, although they remain market *oriented,* and markets play a more important role in their economies than they did in command economies, they are still clearly *mixtures* of market and command elements.

In addition to these common trends *within* industrial societies, there has been a trend of increasing *interdependence* between them. The world today is truly a *global economy.*

Table 10.7 (page 234) provides a glimpse of the degree to which this is the case. It should be noted that the very low *percentage* for the United States does not indicate that it has a low level of international trade, but rather that it has an extraordinarily *huge* economy with a large domestic component (e.g., see Table 9.2 on page 204).

IMPORTANT TERMS

labor intensive	multinational corporation	specialization
primary industry	capital intensive	living standard
command economy	secondary industry	tertiary industry
laissez-faire	market economy	mixed economy
competitive advantage	costs	variable costs
vertical integration	monopoly	oligopoly
interlocking directorate	corporation	limited liability

RECOMMENDED READING

1. The *Statistical Abstract of the United States,* issued annually by the U.S. Department of Commerce, Bureau of the Census (http://www.census.gov). A treasure trove of data on the United States with some comparative international statistics.

2. The *Historical Statistics of the United States: Colonial Times to 1970,* also by the U.S. Department of Commerce, Bureau of the Census (http://www.census.gov). Provides a wealth of historical and trend data on the United States. Since the United States passed the industrial "threshold" about 1870–1880, some of these data allow comparisons between a preindustrial and a fully industrialized society. It can be found in the reference section of your library.

3. The *World Development Report* and *World Development Indicators CD-ROM,* issued annually by the World Bank. Presents up-to-date social, demographic, and economic data on a large number of societies at various levels of development. (See also http://www.worldbank.org/data/onlinedatabases/onlinedatabases.html).

4. *The Coming of Post-Industrial Society: A Venture in Social Forecasting,* by Daniel Bell (New York: Basic Books, 1976). Chapter 2 provides a good discussion of the shift from secondary to tertiary industries and its consequences.

QUIZ QUESTIONS

Fill-in-the-Blank

1. Between 1800 and 1997-1999 technological development reduced the labor needed to produce basic agricultural products by about ____ percent.

2. The per capita GNP in the United States is now about ____ times what it was in 1870.

3. Production that is based largely on the work of people is called _____ intensive, whereas production that is based on the work of machines and money is called _____ intensive.

4. Industries that produce raw materials are _____ industries, those that produce finished products such as furniture and automobiles are _____ industries, and those that provide services such as education and government are _____ industries.

5. In 1840 most people in the United States were employed in _____ industries; today most people are employed in _____ industries.

6. An economy in which the government or an elite determines what is produced is called a/an _____ economy, whereas one in which producers and consumers freely exchange their goods is called a/an _____ economy.

7. A capitalist economy in which the government plays a minimal role is called _____.

8. As a "rule of thumb" an industry is considered oligopolistic when ____ or fewer firms account for ____ percent or more of production.

9. A corporation embodies the principle of _____ liability.

True or False

10. Although the total quantities of energy and materials consumed in industrial societies have increased, the *per capita* amounts consumed have generally declined.

11. Today more people are employed in blue-collar occupations than in white-collar occupations.

12. Large companies are likely to have the greatest competitive advantage in industries where a large proportion of costs are *fixed.*

13. The U.S. government controls and spends a larger percentage of national income than most other western industrial democracies.

14. McDonald's is a good example of capital-intensive production.

15. Levels of union membership are slightly higher in the United States and Canada than they are in Sweden and Finland.

16. The majority of women in industrial societies are employed in the paid labor force.

17. A production cost that *increases* with sales volume is known as a variable cost.

18. Breakfast cereals and breweries are clear examples of oligopolistic industries.

19. The economies of advanced industrial societies are either pure market or pure planned; they are not mixtures of these two elements.

20. The average industrial government spent about half as much in 2005 as it did in 1870.

21. Today there is more trade between societies than ever before.

22. Canada, Switzerland, and Sweden are advanced industrial societies.

23. Industrial societies consume more than ten times the energy per capita as do contemporary (industrializing) horticultural societies.

Multiple Choice

24. Between 1800 and 1997–99 the labor required to produce a given quantity of wheat, corn, cotton, and chicken declined by about:
    a) 56 percent
    b) 72 percent
    c) 85 percent
    d) 99 percent
    e) none of the above

25. Over the past 100 years or so in the United States, the standard of living has:
    a) decreased dramatically
    b) decreased a little bit
    c) increased dramatically
    d) increased a little bit
    e) none of the above

26. The fastest growing segment of the occupational structure of industrial societies is employment in _____ industries.
    a) primary
    b) secondary
    c) tertiary
    d) quarternary
    e) manufacturing

27. Because of the dramatic growth in services, most people today are employed in _____ -collar occupations.
    a) blue
    b) white
    c) striped
    d) iron
    e) no

28. The three kinds of economies discussed in Chapter 10 are _____, _____, and _____.

    a) submarket, market, and supermarket
    b) subsistence, market, and command
    c) western, eastern, and middle eastern
    d) nonproductive, productive, and sufficient
    e) none of the above

29. Which of the following is *not* a problem associated with a purely free market?
    a) child labor
    b) long working hours
    c) growing competitive advantage and monopoly
    d) unsafe working conditions
    e) none of the above (all of these are problems)

30. The principal of limited liability applies to:
    a) state-owned enterprises
    b) modern corporations
    c) the gross domestic product
    d) labor-intensive industries
    e) oligopoly

31. According to the text, control of large capitalist corporations is exercised by:
    a) managers and the government
    b) stockholders and the people
    c) investors and philanthropists
    d) the CIA and FBI
    e) none of the above

32. Economies that are *mixtures* of market and command elements:
    a) cannot last very long (they self-destruct)
    b) have never developed in industrial societies
    c) are rarely found in the modern world
    d) are called *subsistence* economies
    e) none of the above

33. According to Table 10.6 (p. 230), industrial governments (on average) spent about ___ of their gross domestic products in 2005.
    a) 22 percent
    b) 31 percent
    c) 44 percent
    d) 58 percent
    e) 72 percent

Essay/Study Questions

34. Why has the growth in technological information had such a dramatic effect on industrial societies?

35. Discuss some of the most important economic trends that have occurred in advanced industrial societies. How are their economies different today than they were 100–150 years ago?

36. Open *Human Societies* to page 221 and look at Table 10.2. What important changes, trends, and social problems in the United States do you think are consequences of the employment trends depicted in this table?

37. What are the important differences between *planned* (command) and *market* economies?

38. What special problems/flaws does a (laissez-faire) market economy have?

39. What does it mean to say that competitive market economies have a tendency to *self-destruct*?

40. What are some of the important differences between an oligopoly and a monopoly?

41. Why did the development of industrial technology produce such a dramatic rise in the standard of living when previous technological revolutions (e.g., horticulture, agriculture) produced little, if any, benefit for the average member of society?

42. Why have the service industries (tertiary sector) grown so much with advancing industrialization? Will such growth continue?

NOTES

[1] The industrial societies on page 216, which are the focus of Chapters 10–13, are the most productive societies in Table 9.3—those with 2006 per capita GNPs of $10,000 or more (in 2000 U.S. dollars).

[2] The process whereby increasing technological development first produced rapid population growth, and then population stabilization (or even decline), which demographers refer to as the **demographic transition**, is discussed on pages 280–281. One crucial aspect of this process was the dramatic decline in death rates that resulted at first from improved sanitation and nutrition, and later from improved medical technology and practices (see Table 13.1 on page 279).

[3] It is worth emphasizing that "tertiary industries" constitute a "residual" category. Whatever is not clearly extractive or manufacturing is, by default, considered tertiary. As a result, it contains a wide range of industries and occupations—from the highest paid, most rewarding occupations (e.g., medical doctor, lawyer, architect) to the lowest paid, least rewarding occupations (e.g., cafeteria worker, hospital orderly, garbage collector). Therefore, depending on which aspect is focused on, or which is growing the fastest, growth in the tertiary can indicate either an overall *improvement* or a *degradation* of the labor force.

[4] This too has occasionally engendered contradictory reactions and evaluations. White-collar work has traditionally been clean and often challenging or rewarding work; however, with the advent of computers this may be changing. Although computers have reduced much of the tedium and repetitiveness of some work, they have also greatly increased the degree to which workers can be supervised and monitored. Some have argued that the detailed monitoring of "keystrokes" and breaks in activity that computers make possible may have made modern white-collar offices into "electronic sweatshops." Sweatshops were some of the most demanding and dehumanizing workplaces developed in the industrial era.

[5] Even though manufacturing *employment* did not absorb the majority of displaced workers, tertiary industries, since, in large part, they repair and maintain the people and machines in manufacturing, were also concentrated in urban areas.

[6] As we will see in the next chapter, Adam Smith thought government could legitimately play a role in public education and in enforcing contracts. Anything more constituted unwarranted interference and would disrupt the natural forces of the market. Such a system is sometimes referred to as "laissez-faire" capitalism.

[7] Recognize that from a "balance-sheet" point of view, safety laws may be viewed as costly and inefficient. In fact, many companies used to refrain from installing safety equipment on machines because it was *cheaper* to pay the claims of the injured or their widows. In a laissez-faire system, *only* economic factors are considered, and as long as someone is willing to work in the existing conditions, nothing would be done to change them. The citizens of industrial societies have generally decided, however, that in a number of situations purely economic considerations must be subordinated to the need for individual, and public, health and safety.

[8] As we will see in the excursus to Chapter 15, laws restricting pollution and protecting public health have been nonexistent or ineffective in most revolutionary-socialist societies. Because the citizens of such societies were not allowed to organize and address such problems, and because they were struggling so hard to keep up economically with the West, environmental damage was almost literally "swept under the rug" in these societies. We are only now becoming aware of the massive pollution and environmental degradation wrought by the former Soviet Union and communist Eastern Europe.

[9] Note also that, despite the concern and debate over the amount of governmental and welfare expenditures in it, the United States is near the bottom of this list of industrial societies in terms of the amount of social product consumed by the government.

[10] As a "rule of thumb," an industry is considered oligopolistic if four or fewer firms account for 50 percent or more of production in it.

11

Industrial Societies

Ideologies and Polities

CHAPTER SUMMARY

The chapter begins with a discussion of the growth in the information stores of societies in the past 500 years and of how the increasing size of the economic surplus of industrial societies raises the *potential* influence of ideology on the structures and trends of development in industrial societies. Special attention is given to the major tenets of the *new secular* ideologies—**democratic republicanism, capitalism, democratic** and **revolutionary socialism, environmentalism, nationalism, pragmatism,** and **hedonism**. This is followed by an examination of trends in the polities of industrial societies: the trend toward democracy, the development of mass political parties, the increasing role of the mass media (especially television), their greater stability, and the growth in the size of governments and the scope of their powers.

As the information stores of industrial societies have grown, two dominant trends in ideology have emerged: a general decline in the influence of *theistic religions,* and an increase in the influence of *secular ideologies.* This general decline can be seen in Table 11.1, but note how exceptional the United States is in this regard. This is, no doubt, the continuing influence of its historical religious origins.

The secular ideologies that have exercised the greatest influence in the modern era are: (1) **democratic republicanism**, (2) **capitalism**, (3) **democratic** and **revolutionary socialism**, (4) **environmentalism**, (5) **nationalism**, (6) **pragmatism,** and (7) **hedonism**.

Republicanism is an ideology that maintains that government should reflect the interests of, and be responsible to, the people governed. What makes the *democratic* republicanism of industrial societies so unusual and so revolutionary, however, is its advocacy that *all,* or *most,* people should be represented. In the past, republican governments were unapologetically *oligarchical* or *elitist*; the government was (rightfully) thought to represent only the select few who were thought worthy or capable of self-government. The belief that the average person, or the total population, should be represented was indeed revolutionary, and, as we will see shortly, it has had a profound effect on politics in industrial societies.

The ideology of **capitalism** was systematized and eloquently argued in Adam Smith's *Wealth of Nations,* first published in 1776. His basic argument was that although people are most strongly motivated by self-interest, if they are allowed to pursue this self-interest unhindered, the end result will be *good.* Self-interest and the pursuit of profit will reliably motivate people to produce the things that other people want and need, as long as people are allowed to produce, buy, and sell whatever they want. The baker produces bread not because he is altruistically motivated to feed the hungry, but because he can make money by doing it.

Furthermore, Smith argued, in a free market, the price of a commodity reflects both the demand (need) for it, and its supply. If demand is high and supply low, the price will be high, and, as a result, the *incentive* to produce it will be high. As this incentive stimulates production, supply increases and the price and the incentive to produce it will fall. Thus, according to Smith, if the market is not interfered with, it will be as if an "invisible hand" magically balances supply and demand. Anything that upsets the balance between supply and demand (e.g., an increase in a need, development of a "new" need, a shortfall in production) *automatically* triggers forces that will restore it; in the end, virtually every human need for which people are willing to pay or work to have satisfied will be met.

Although Smith's ideas are primarily concerned with economics, they clearly have implications for government and society. Perhaps most important is the economic and moral justification they provide for self-interest (selfishness) and for individual autonomy and liberty. For surprisingly, he argued, the exercise of individualism and self-interest would not increase vice and misery, as many believed, but would actually promote happiness and well-being. In fact, the worst mistake a society or government could make, from Smith's view, would be to interfere with human "selfishness" and the natural operation of the free market.

Socialism maintains that because production is a *social* process, the productive process ought to be controlled by, and the wealth it produces owned by, society; that is, by all the people. Nonetheless, there are important differences between *democratic* and *revolutionary* socialism.

Democratic socialism assumes that since its goals have appeal for all working people, and the great majority of people in industrial societies work, it can achieve power through *democratic* (electoral) means. Where it has successfully done so (e.g., Sweden), it has promoted what is known as the **welfare state,** a (benevolent) government that (re)distributes income for the benefit of workers and provides a number of services for the population at little or no cost (e.g., health care).

Revolutionary socialism, as articulated in the writings of Karl Marx and Frederick Engels, maintained that only through a revolution, and probably a violent one at that, could the **proletariat** take control of society and make it communist.[1] In Lenin's writings and in a society where political activities were outlawed by the state, this became a justification for a secretive, *elitist,* and totalitarian system of control. As a result, Marx's ideals, based on an enlightenment view of inherently good and perfectible human nature, became the call words of, and justification for, highly centralized, dictatorial governments that, like parents with young children, often justified their actions as being good for their charges, even if they were not knowledgeable or mature enough to see that for themselves.[2] We will discuss the social and political consequences of revolutionary socialism in more detail in an excursus to Chapter 14, "Marxist Societies as Natural Experiments."

In addition to these divergent ideologies, three ideologies have exerted a more general influence on industrial societies—**nationalism, pragmatism,** and **hedonism**.

Nationalism has been a force in many societies, creating a sense of national identity that transcends the local, regional, and ethnic identities of populations. In fact, it has been so successful in so many industrial societies that it is generally noticed only where it is absent—that is, in situations where despite prolonged membership in a single polity, ethnic, racial and culturally distinct groups *do not* recognize a common national identity. Northern Ireland and the Basques of Spain are newsworthy examples, as is the apparent ethnic disintegration now occurring in Bosnia and the former Soviet Union.

Although not adopted as a systematic philosophy as it was articulated by William James, **pragmatism** has been a profound influence on a number of very different kinds of societies. Certainly, the idea that people should be concerned with "what works" when making political and economic choices is widespread among industrial and industrializing societies.

Finally, because of the tremendous productivity and growing affluence of advanced industrial societies, **hedonism**, the pursuit of pleasure, has had a pervasive and growing impact. This is perhaps best illustrated by the vast incomes, attention, and status accorded to entertainers, "celebrities," and star athletes in the United States today.

A striking feature of all of these secular ideologies is their shared assumption that *human destiny and future societal development may be subject to human control.* Whether this is a valid insight or a phantom dream remains to be seen.[3]

Polities are the institutional systems by which decisions are made and populations are governed in societies. The "campfire democracies" of hunting and gathering bands were probably the *most democratic* polities ever developed by humans. In them everyone had a chance to express his/her opinion, and, since one was likely to have relatives in surrounding societies, it was often possible to escape the consequences of a decision one disagreed with by simply picking up and moving to a neighboring society. The increasing size, social differentiation, and concentration of resources and power in elites that followed the adoption of horticulture and then agriculture, however, increasingly *restricted* participation in decision making to an ever smaller proportion of the population—the governing elite—and the sedentary nature of cultivation made moving difficult if not impossible.

It is thus something of a surprise that this trend has apparently *reversed* itself in the polities of industrial societies. This can be seen clearly in Figure 11.1 (page 248), which traces the extension of the right to vote (the franchise) in western Europe as it industrialized. Although far from making them *pure* democracies, these and other institutional changes that followed the Industrial Revolution transformed most industrial societies from *oligarchical* to *democratic* republics.[4]

A number of factors contributed to this trend: (1) the Protestant Reformation and its encouragement of (mass) literacy,[5] (2) the democratizing influence of "frontiers," (3) advancing industrialization's increasing demand for skilled, educated workers, (4) the emergence of mass media of communication (daily newspapers, serialized fiction, and later radio and television), and (5) the tremendous growth of urban populations.

Although it is easy to document extension of the vote and the development of mass communication, it is much more difficult to assess the degree and effectiveness of citizen participation in government. In fact, this too should be considered a *variable.* Nonetheless, it cannot be assumed that it is even possible for every citizen to participate in decision-making in industrial societies, or that their participation will be *equally* influential or effective. There are a number of *inescapable limits* on the political participation of citizens of large complex societies.[6]

Dahl and Tufte's[7] discussion of "Glaucon's problem" provides a very useful example of one of the basic constraints on participation—time. Taking the Athenian Senate as his focus, Glaucon asked how long it would take a quorum—6,000 citizens—to debate an important issue such as whether or not to go to war.[8]

Some simple arithmetic shows that if every senator is given fifteen minutes to state his view, it would take 150 days of meeting ten hours a day (or 62.5 days meeting twenty-four hours a day) to complete the discussion. Furthermore, if you allow it to be more of a *debate* by giving each senator an additional fifteen minutes to respond to the view of *each* of the 5,999 other senators, it would take more than 3,000 years of meeting ten hours a day, 300 days a year (or 1,027 years if they met twenty-four hours a day, 365 days a year) just to complete the debate! And this is the amount of time necessary for 6,000 people to conclude a debate. Imagine how long it would take to have such a discussion in industrial communities that consist of *hundreds of thousands or millions* of people!

Moreover, even if some of these limits could be expanded by modern technology, the fact that most people lack the necessary expertise and the time to research and ponder issues would remain. Few people have the training or "spare time" to master the requisite information for any *one* of the dozens or hundreds of issues routinely confronted by the governments of complex industrial societies, let alone for *all* of them.

All of this, Michels argued, necessitates restrictions on citizen participation and the development of systems of "representation."[9] But although systems of representation and limits on participation solve the problem of limited "reaction time" and limited expertise, they create new problems. One of the most important is the possibility they provide for a significant divergence or "gap" to develop between the views and behavior of the representatives and the people they supposedly represent.

In addition, they may also endow organized "special interests" with disproportionate influence on legislation and government policies. Organized interest groups that vote in blocs are more likely to get the attention of politicians than are unorganized individuals, even if the latter are more numerous. Furthermore, successful campaigns in large industrial societies are expensive, and politicians are compelled to respond to individuals and organizations that can provide the finances and other resources needed to conduct successful campaigns.[10]

Yet, if the governments of western industrial market societies fall short of their democratic ideals, the situation was even worse in revolutionary-socialist societies. As the excursus to Chapter 14 shows, they did not even remotely resemble the stateless utopias or "worker's paradises" envisioned by Karl Marx. However, as recent events indicate, they too appear to be experiencing something of a "democratic trend."

Therefore, recognition of the *inescapable limits* on democracy in complex societies need not lead to apathy and cynicism, since, as even Michels noted, recognition of the impossibility of *pure* democracy should lead to a better appreciation of *degrees* of democracy that are possible. If a citizenry is aware of the limitations on democracy, they are in a better position to appreciate the need for limitations on government power and for the safeguarding of citizens' rights. As Winston Churchill once observed, "Democracy is the worst form of government—except for all of those other forms that have been tried from time to time."

Despite these common trends and great similarities, however, there are some interesting and important differences among industrial societies. One is the varying degree to which political behavior is influenced by social class. In some societies social class and economic issues are the overriding political issues; in others, although they are not irrelevant, they are simply *some* of *many* political issues confronting the citizenry. Tables 11.2 and 11.3 (on pages 256 and 257) show the connection between social class position and political party affiliation in a number of industrial societies. Table 11.2 shows that in Sweden most "working class" people (74 percent) support the Socialist or Communist Party, whereas relatively few (30 percent) of the "upper" and "middle" classes do. A simple way to summarize the *strength* of this connection or association between social class and party affiliation is to take the *difference* between these percentages (74 percent − 30 percent = 44). It indicates that members of the working class are 44 percent *more likely* to support the Socialist or Communist parties than are the members of other classes. This is a *strong* relationship; social class is thus strongly associated with political party affiliation in Sweden.[11]

Table 11.3, which presents the percentage differences for eleven industrial societies (note the figure of forty-four for Sweden), but not the percentages they were computed from, shows that the strength of this relationship varies considerably. It is very strong in the Scandinavian countries (Finland, Norway, Denmark, and Sweden) and very weak in the United States and Canada. Differences in the strength of association appear to reflect differences in the degree of religious and ethnic heterogeneity in these societies; it is generally strong in *homogeneous* societies and weak in *heterogeneous* societies.[12] In ethnically, racially, and religiously homogeneous societies, economic differences are the *only* things that divide people and animate politics; in ethnically, racially, and religiously heterogeneous populations, economic and social class differences are only *some* of *many* issues that divide people and animate politics. Furthermore, people divided on one issue, may be united on others. Such cross-cutting differences, therefore, are more conducive to compromise and incremental change than to confrontation and violence. Democratic forms of participation (e.g., voting), together with the increasing heterogeneity of industrial societies, make the politics of industrial societies much less violent than they were in agrarian societies, or than they often are in contemporary nondemocratic societies.[13]

IMPORTANT TERMS

democratic/oligarchical	republicanism	theistic religion
secular ideology	capitalism	communism
democratic/revolutionary	socialism	environmentalism
oligarchical/democratic	republics	proletariat
pragmatism	citizens	subjects
mass media	franchise	mass parties
homogeneity	heterogeneity	totalitarianism
brokerage-type parties	special-interest group	bureaucracy
multiparty democracy	pacifism	polity
green parties	percentage difference	welfare state

RECOMMENDED READING

1. *The Worldly Philosophers,* by Robert Heilbroner (NY: Time Books, 1961). Provides excellent, short introductions to the theories of Adam Smith and Karl Marx. See also his more recent book, *Marx: For and Against* (NY: Norton, 1980).

2. *The Marx-Engels Reader,* by Robert C. Tucker, 3d ed. (NY: Norton, 1978). A representative selection of the important writings of Marx and Engels with a very good introduction and chapter synopses by Tucker.

3. *The Immanent Utopia: From Marxism on the State to the State of Marxism,* by Axel van den Berg (Princeton, NJ: Princeton University Press, 1988). As the title implies, and excellent critique of the Marxist theory of the state and the state of Marxism.

4. *The Science of Culture,* by Leslie White (NY: Farrar, Straus, 1949). A collection of this outspoken anthropologist's essays on human societies and the possibility of a scientific understanding of them. All are interesting and worth reading, but most relevant to this chapter is Chapter XII, "Man's Control over Civilization: An Anthropocentric Illusion." The book cannot be bought (it is out of print), but your library should have a copy.

5. *The British Political Elite,* by W. L. Guttsman (London: Macgibbon and Kee, 1963); and *The English Ruling Class,* edited by W. L. Guttsman (London: Weidenfeld and

Nicolson, 1969). Both contain fascinating data on British political elites of an earlier era.

6. *The Irony of Democracy,* by Thomas R. Dye and L. Harmon Zeigler (Belmont, CA: Wadsworth, 1993). Examines the elitist nature of politics in the United States from its founding to the present.

7. *Size and Democracy,* by Robert Dahl and Edward Tufte (Stanford, CA: Stanford University Press, 1973). An excellent discussion and empirical exploration of the ways in which large size limits participation of citizens in government.

8. *Political Parties,* by Robert Michels (NY: Free Press, 1968); and *The Ruling Class,* by Gaetano Mosca (NY: McGraw-Hill, 1939). Two very good sources on the limitations of participation in large societies. Michels provides a classic analysis of the problems that arise in efforts to implement socialist ideals, using the socialist parties of western Europe as test cases. Mosca made one of the most successful predictions in modern social science when he forecast in the 1890s the nature of the polities and stratification systems of modern Marxist-Leninist societies.

9. *Liberal Fascism: The Secret History of the American Left from Mussolini to the Politics of Meaning, by Jonah Goldberg* (NY: Doubleday, 2007). Goldberg presents a well-documented and cogent argument that Fascism and Naziism are variants of socialism.

10. U.S. Department of Commerce, Bureau of the Census, *Statistical Abstract of the United States* and the *Historical Statistics of the United States, Colonial Times to 1970* (http://www.census.gov). Important sources of basic information on the United States. Paperback almanacs, readily available in libraries and at supermarkets and bookstores, also present up-to-date information on governments and voting.

11. *The Statesman's Yearbook* (annual from New York: St. Martin's Press); *The Political Handbook of the World* (annual from Binghamton, NY: CSA Publications); and *The World Factbook* (*http://www.cia.gov/cia/publications/factbook/*) provide invaluable information on the governments and politics of nations of the world. Check the reference section of your library to see if it has them.

12. Annual editions of the *Gallup Poll: Public Opinion* (Wilmington, DL: Scholarly Resources) provide the results of recent opinion polls and note long-term trends in opinion in the United States. *Index to International Public Opinion* (Westport, CT: Greenwood Press) periodically presents similar information for other nations of the world. Check the reference section of your library to see if it has them.

QUIZ QUESTIONS

Fill-in-the-Blank

1. Judaism, Christianity, and Islam are examples of _____.

2. Ideologies that are not centered on belief in a god (or gods) are known as _____ ideologies.

3. "Government of the people, by the people, and for the people" is an example of _____ republicanism.

4. The moral philosopher who systematized and popularized capitalism was _____.

5. The welfare state is associated with _____ socialism.

6. The spiritual father of revolutionary socialism is _____.

7. The development of a sense of common identity among different people and across different regions of a society is known as _____.

8. William James is associated with the development of _____.

9. In most agrarian societies the people are referred to as _____, whereas in most industrial societies they are referred to as _____.

10. Environmentalists, labor unions, and industries are examples of _____ groups.

11. When it was founded, the United States was a/an _____ republic, whereas today it is a/an _____ republic.

12. The _____ difference summarizes the relationship between two variables.

13. The movement against the Catholic Church in Europe that gave rise to a number of new denominations of Christianity (e.g., Lutheran, Presbyterian, Baptist, Methodist) is called the _____.

True or False

14. The influence of theistic religions has generally increased in industrial societies.

15. *Oligarchical* republicanism is a new ideology that first emerged in industrial societies.

16. Pragmatism advocates the "dictatorship of the proletariat."

17. The belief that a society should be governed by a small group of its wealthiest people is associated with democratic republicanism.

18. According to the text, "power-brokerage" parties are firmly committed to clear ideological principles.

19. In recent years "environmentalism" has developed a number of features that parallel those of traditional Christianity.

20. Occupational class plays a stronger role in politics in the United States than it does in most Scandinavian societies.

21. At its founding, the United States was an oligarchical republic.

22. Politics in industrial societies are less violent than they were in agrarian.

Multiple Choice

23. In general the influence of secular ideologies has _____ in industrial societies.
    a) increased
    b) declined
    c) gone up and down in cycles
    d) drifted randomly
    e) none of the above

24. Democratic socialism is associated with:
    a) the welfare state
    b) the dictatorship of the proletariat
    c) Marx, Engels, and Lenin
    d) Adam Smith
    e) none of the above

25. Which of the following is a secular ideology that first developed in industrial societies?
    a) Buddhism
    b) Christianity
    c) Islam
    d) Pragmatism
    e) all of the above

26. Which of the following is a theistic religion?
    a) Marxism
    b) Leninism
    c) Pragmatism
    d) Islam
    e) none of the above

27. According to Marx, _____ is the root cause of most of the evils of industrial societies.
    a) greed
    b) private property
    c) technology
    d) secular ideology
    e) theistic religion

28. One of the primary differences between capitalism and socialism is the extent to which:
    a) the economy is controlled by government
    b) the society depends on industrial technology for subsistence
    c) the population is literate
    d) a university education is considered valuable by the population
    e) none of the above

29. According to the book, the governments of industrial societies are distinctive because they:
    a) collect taxes
    b) treat their governed as "subjects"
    c) benefit advantaged groups more than disadvantaged groups
    d) are likely to be multiparty democracies
    e) none of the above

30. *Pure* democracy—equal participation by everyone in all decisions—is:
    a) found in most, but not all, industrial societies
    b) possible only in the largest, most technologically advanced societies
    c) found only in western (capitalist) industrial societies
    d) found only in North America (i.e., Canada and the United States)
    e) impossible in industrial societies

31. Which of the following was *not* a factor that contributed to the "democratic trend" in industrial societies?
    a) the increasing need for unskilled labor in advanced industrial societies
    b) the conquest of the New World
    c) mass literacy
    d) the mass media
    e) none of the above (all of these fostered democracy)

32. "Brokerage-type" parties are generally found in:
    a) revolutionary-socialist societies
    b) welfare states
    c) democratic-socialist societies
    d) eastern European societies
    e) none of the above

33. Social class is most likely to be a strong influence on political party preference in societies that are:
    a) industrial
    b) poor
    c) ethnically and religiously homogeneous
    d) ethnically and religiously heterogeneous
    e) none of the above

34. In which of the following societies does social class have a relatively *strong* influence on political party preference?
    a) Finland
    b) the United States
    c) France
    d) Australia
    e) Canada

35. Which of the following is generally true of the governments of all industrial societies?
    a) They have grown in size.
    b) They have taken on more functions.

    c) They have grown in power and influence.
    d) all of the above
    e) none of the above

36. In general, the greater the economic development of a society, the more _____ its politics.
    a) violent
    b) unpredictable
    c) polarized
    d) totalitarian
    e) stable

37. The secular ideology that emphasizes the pursuit of pleasure is called:
    a) pleasureism
    b) pragmatism
    c) environmentalism
    d) hedonism
    e) none of the above

Essay/Study Questions

38. Why has the influence of theistic religion generally declined in industrial societies?

39. What are some of the new secular ideologies that have developed in industrial societies? What are some of their important *differences*? What are their important *similarities*?

40. What are the similarities and differences between *oligarchical* and *democratic* republicanism?

41. What are the similarities and differences between *democratic* and *revolutionary* socialism?

42. Why would you expect differences in ideology to have a greater impact on industrial societies than they had on agrarian societies?

43. What has been the most important political trend in the majority of industrial societies?

44. Name two of the factors responsible for the growth of democracy in modern industrial societies.

45. What are some of the ways that the Protestant Reformation has affected politics in western societies?

46. What are some of the trends common to all industrial polities?

47. How do ethnic and religious homogeneity/heterogeneity affect politics in industrial societies?

48. Why are the politics of Canada and the United States less clearly focused on issues of social class than are the politics of Europe and Scandinavia?

49. What are the primary objectives of brokerage-type parties in industrial societies?

50. Why have the governments of industrial societies grown so much with advancing industrialization?

51. Are the governments of industrial societies more or less stable, and their politics more or less violent, than those of agrarian societies?

52. How would you explain the nearly universal extension of the right to vote in industrial societies?

NOTES

[1] The term *proletariat,* which originally denoted the lowest class in ancient Roman society, is used by Marx and Engels to refer to those in industrial societies who do not own private property. It is important to realize, however, that **private property**, which Marx thought was the root cause of all injustice, vice, and misery in industrial societies, refers to ownership of the productive machinery (capital goods) of a society (e.g., factories, machines, investment assets); it does not mean *personal possessions* such as clothing, homes, automobiles, and the like. When Marx is decrying and sounding the death knell of private property, he is not proposing or predicting the end of personal possessions in communist societies. In fact, if anything, he believed that more people would have more things in such societies. However, a more generous distribution of possessions was less important to Marx than was his belief that such a society would be more just, and its production process less a violation of human nature, than capitalist societies.

[2] The idea that people can be unaware of their own "true" interests (have a "false consciousness" of their situation and needs) and that scientists or government officials, therefore, should be empowered to do what is "objectively" best for, or to, them, even if they object and attempt to resist, is clearly one of the most dangerous and potentially exploitative political ideas to emerge in any era.

[3] The renowned anthropologist Leslie White called the (false) human belief that we could control the development of culture "an anthropocentric illusion."

[4] As the text points out, it is very important to recognize that democracy is *variable.* In fact, it is something of a misnomer to call any industrial society a "democracy," since, for reasons we will discuss later, no large industrial society can be purely democratic (allow equal participation by all citizens in all collective decisions); however, some societies are clearly *more* democratic (allow greater citizen participation) than others.

[5] One of the key Protestant "reforms" was the idea that individuals should be taught to read so that they would be able to read the Bible for themselves.

[6] Robert Michels' classic, *Political Parties* (NY: Free Press, 1962), is probably the most comprehensive study of the features of organization that make it *impossible* for large organizations and societies to be *pure* democracies. One of his key examples is the fact that the socialist parties of western Europe, which argued that, if empowered, they would make *societies* true democracies, were *themselves* not democratically governed! Michels called his finding that democracy is impossible in large-scale organizations the "iron law of oligarchy." It is one of the few sociological findings that is strong enough to be considered a *law.*

[7] *Size and Democracy,* by Robert Dahl and Edward Tufte (Stanford, CA: Stanford University Press, 1973).

[8] It is important to note that although many societies in Greece were "democracies" for their *citizens,* fewer than 10 percent of their populations were citizens!

[9] In addition to the clear limits that the size and complexity of industrial societies place on citizen participation, Mauk Mulder has presented experimental evidence that the effects of participation are not equally beneficial. For instance, when managers and workers jointly discuss issues before making decisions, the managers typically persuade workers; workers do not persuade managers. Even more disheartening are the results of his experiments, which indicate that the mere *appearance* of expertise is influential. He has shown experimentally that if some people *appear* to know more than others (even if they really don't), others are more likely to abandon their independent judgment in order to agree with the "expert." See: Mauk Mulder and Henk Wilke, "Participation and Power Equalization," *Organizational Behavior and Human Performance* 5 (1970): 430–48; and Mauk Mulder, "Power Equalization through Participation?" *Administrative Science Quarterly* 16 (9171): 31–38.

[10] Note the Gallup Poll results discussed on page 259.

[11] A useful "rule of thumb" regarding the strength of associations indicated by percentage differences is the following:

  10 or less: no relationship
  10 to 30: a weak to moderate relationship
  30 to 50: a moderate to strong relationship
  50 or more: a very strong relationship

[12] An exception to this general principle occurs when religious, ethnic, racial, and economic differences *coincide,* as in South Africa or Northern Ireland. When they do, differences *reinforce* one another and polarize the population into two distinct groups with no overlap and no common ground. As recent history indicates, because there is no common ground and little basis for compromise, politics in such societies is generally confrontational and often violent.

[13] The fact that *any kind* of participation tends to make people feel better about their government helps to explain why one-party totalitarian states periodically take the trouble to stage elections even though there is often only one candidate for each office and the ballot is far from secret.

12

Industrial Societies

Social Stratification

CHAPTER SUMMARY

The chapter opens with a discussion of the long-term trend of growing complexity in the stratification of societies and of the increasingly "positive sum" nature of stratification in industrial societies. It then examines in more detail the levels and trends in political, income, wealth, occupational, educational, racial and ethnic, and age and sex inequality in industrial societies. This is followed by a brief discussion of the increasing opportunities for upward social mobility in industrial societies. The chapter closes with a discussion of two basic trends in equality in the industrial era—the trend of declining inequality and rising standards of living *within* advanced industrial societies, and the growing gap *between* them and the nonindustrialized societies in the world system.

Agrarian societies were probably the most highly stratified societies humans ever developed. Not only were there great disparities among individuals and classes of people on any *single* dimension of ranking (e.g., wealth, power, education, prestige), but there was also a very strong correlation across dimensions. Thus, if one was high or low on a particular dimension of inequality (e.g., power), one was also likely to be similarly high or low on others (e.g., wealth). Inequality was thus *compounded* across dimensions of stratification.

The situation is much more complicated in industrial societies. There are many more dimensions of ranking in them, there are more levels or gradations on each dimension, and the correlation across dimensions (although still rather high) is weaker. Statements about the degree of, or trend in, inequality in industrial societies, therefore, may differ for each dimension. As a result, we must consider the dimensions of power, income, wealth, and occupation separately.[1] We must also consider, despite ideological—and in some cases legal—prohibitions, the extent to which *ascribed* characteristics (e.g., sex, race, age) continue to influence access to, and control of, valued resources (e.g., wealth, income, education) in industrial societies.

Political, economic, and social elites in industrial societies are clearly more influential and advantaged than the *average citizen,* but political stratification is much less severe in the industrial societies than in agrarian. A key reason for this is the fact that there are a *number* of elites in western industrial societies (e.g., economic, political, social, educational)—who are at times in conflict or in competition with one another for public support. *No single elite* has the power to decide or dominate all, or most, resource allocations in industrial societies—for example, questions of employment, book publication, imprisonment, education, residence, and the like.[2] Furthermore, the existence of competitive markets, a "free" press, and competing political parties makes these elites much more accountable for their actions than were elites in agrarian societies.

Also, although a substantial number of the wealthiest people in the world live in the United States (see Table 12.1 on page 264), there is also less income inequality in industrial societies than in the agrarian societies of the past, or contemporary nonindustrial societies.

A simple way to judge the *degree* of inequality in income distributions is to compare them to what they would be if income were *equally* divided. If income were distributed *equally*, the highest-earning 20 percent would earn exactly 20 percent of the total income, and the lowest-earning 40 percent would earn exactly 40 percent of the total income. Although this is clearly an unrealistic expectation, it provides a *benchmark* for judging the *degree* of inequality that exists. The more the share of the top 20 percent exceeds 20 percent, and the more the share of the bottom 40 percent falls short of 40 percent, the *greater* the inequality—the top earners are getting more than their proportionate share, and the bottom earners are getting less. In addition, a summary of the relative departures from equality in *both* shares can be computed by calculating the ratio of the income share of top earners to that of the bottom earners. If income is equally distributed, the ratio will be 20 to 40 (1:2, ½, or 0.5).

With this in mind, consider the data in Table 12.2 (page 265) on the distributions of incomes in advanced industrial societies and the average for nonindustrial societies. All the ratios in Table 12.2 depart markedly from the 0.5 that would indicate perfect equality. They range from a low of 1.4 to a high of 3.4. There is thus considerable income inequality in *all* industrial societies, and the degree of income inequality varies substantially among these societies. Among industrial societies, the United States, Israel, and Portugal have some of the highest levels of inequality; Japan, Slovenia, and Finland have the lowest. Nonetheless, even the income distributions of the United States, Israel, and Portugal are *more equal* than the *average* contemporary nonindustrial society whose ratio is 2.9, or, for that matter, the typical agrarian society of the past where the top 2 percent claimed half or more of the total income.

Furthermore, as Figure 12.1 (page 266) indicates, income inequality has *declined* somewhat in the United States over the past seventy years or so. The shape of the curve shows that income inequality declined dramatically between 1929 and the end of World War II—the share of the top 20 percent declined, and that of the bottom 40 percent increased—then it leveled off, before starting to increase in the 1970s and 1980s. This reversal bears watching. It may signal a reversal in this long-term trend of declining inequality, or it may simply reflect a temporary deviation from it. In the meantime, it is important to note that, despite recent increases, income inequality in the United States is today is still *lower* than it was seventy years ago. It is also worth noting that average per capita household incomes have increased—even during the recent period of increasing income inequality—largely because households and families are smaller today, and more of their members are working. We will examine the changing size and incomes of families in more detail in the next chapter (e.g., Table 13.3 on page 285, and Figure 13.2 on page 290).

Figure 12.2 (page 268) shows the trend in the concentration of wealth for a somewhat longer period. It indicates that, with few periods of exception, there has been a sharp and steady decline in the share of wealth owned by the wealthiest 1 percent of individuals.[3]

Given their relatively short attention span, the media often direct attention only to immediate (i.e., one- or two-year) changes in wealth and income.[4] Failure to locate short-term changes in their long-term context can leave the mistaken impression that short-term increases are signs of a continuing long-term trend of increasing income or wealth inequality. When they take a longer perspective, they sometimes (wittingly or unwittingly) choose an unusual level for their starting point. For instance, if you cover the left half of figure 12.1, and look only at the trend since 1970, you would get the impression that income inequality steadily and substantially increases with industrialization. If you consider the entire figure, you realize that although current levels of income inequality may indeed be high and rising, it was *unusually low* in the mid-1970s. Over the full period there is no evidence of a long-term *increase* in income inequality. At worst, it shows that income inequality is nearly as great as it was eighty years ago; it did not start out high then and get steadily greater ever since.[5]

The occupational structure has changed dramatically with advancing industrialization. There has been substantial growth in white-collar occupations and declines in farming and blue-collar occupations (see Table 12.3 on page 268). For many workers, but certainly not all, this has improved their working and living conditions.[6] It has also increased the need for advanced education, making educational differences perhaps the single most important factor affecting most people's access to income and other social rewards.

Despite a general trend in industrial societies toward the greater importance of "achievement" in the allocation of social rewards and resources, ascribed characteristics such as age, sex, and race continue to have measurable associations with people's access to resources and social goods. Older men have dominated politics and economics, women continue to earn less than men, and even today black families earn less than white families.

For example, in 1959 the average black family earned about 52 percent of what the average white family earned; today they earn about 60 percent. It is important to note, however, that one of the key reasons for the persistence of this gap in earnings has been the growth in the number of black *female-headed* households. Today, more than half (53 percent) of all African-American families are female-headed (up from 28 percent in 1970), and 68.8 percent of African American births are to unmarried women (up from 38 percent in 1970).[7] This large proportion of female-headed families pulls the African American family income average down.[8]

If we compare *individual* men and women, however, we find evidence of much more improvement and closing of the gap. In 1940 black men made only about 41 percent of what white men earned; today they earn more than 70 percent, and, in recent years, young black men entering the labor force have earned more than 80 percent of what their white cohorts earn. And, whereas black women earned only 36 percent of what white women earned in 1940, today they earn more than 94 percent of what white women earn.

Perhaps even more striking is the trend depicted in Figure 12.4 (page 271). It shows that the percentage of African Americans in middle-class occupations is more than *five times* greater than it was half a century ago. Rates of home ownership for African Americans are also now at record highs, more than double what they were in 1940, and wealth holdings have increased substantially.

The unemployment rate for blacks, however, is still about twice that of whites. Thus, despite considerable improvement, economic differences between the races persist.

Likewise, despite progress, women's incomes continue to trail men's in industrial societies. It is worth emphasizing, however, that most of the difference in men's and women's incomes is *not* a result of women being paid less for the same job, but of the continuing concentration of women in low paying service sector jobs.[9] We will have more to say about the occupational differences and income gap in the next chapter, but for now it is worth noting that there has been considerable movement toward greater equality in the past 100 years.

For all people with income, the average for women in advanced industrial societies today is about 63 percent, ranging from a low of 45 percent in Japan to a high of 81 percent in Sweden (see Table 12.4 on page 273). With ratios of 64 and 63, respectively, Canada and the United States are about in the middle.

For women and men who are employed full time, the gap has closed more dramatically and is closer to parity.[10] In 1890, the ratio of women's to men's incomes was about 50 percent; today it is about 77 percent (e.g., see the top line of Figure 12.5 on page 274). For younger women (ages 18 to 24) with college degrees, the ratio is even closer—90 percent.[11]

Women's participation in politics has also been increasing in recent decades. The percentage of parliamentary seats held by women has more than doubled since 1975, and more that 40 percent of the seats in Nordic countries are now held by women. Moreover, Norway and Germany recently elected their first female prime ministers.

In the next chapter we will explore further some of the complex interactions among industrial technologies and economies, family life, and women's opportunities outside the home. "Vertical social mobility" is a term sociologists use to denote changes in status that occur either in one's lifetime (final position compared to first job) or across generations (sons compared to fathers, or daughter to mothers). In Chapter 7 we noted that there was not much mobility in agrarian societies, and what there was tended to be downward. This has been reversed in industrial societies. There is much more total movement, and much of it is upward.

For example, two recent ten-year studies by the Treasury Department showed that more than 60 percent of households in the very lowest income category at the start of the studies, were in a higher category 10 years later, and more than 7 percent of them had actually moved to the very highest income category (e.g., see the discussion on page 267, and Table 12.3 on page 268). Furthermore, despite the persistence of differential advantages and access by race, class, and gender, most of this mobility is tied in some way to individual "achievement" (e.g., greater education).

The "quality of life" in industrial societies is also considerably better than it is in nonindustrial societies (e.g., see Table 12.5 on page 277). In fact, based on their average index scores, advanced industrial societies would earn an "A" (95), and nonindustrial societies would earn a "D–" (61).

Finally, despite the movement toward greater income equality *within* industrial societies, there has been an increase in the inequality *between* contemporary industrial and nonindustrial societies. The income gap between rich and poor *societies* has actually grown. We will examine some of the causes and consequences of this in Chapter 14.

IMPORTANT TERMS

zero-sum	positive-sum	quality of life
ascribed/achieved characteristics	income ratio	caste
vertical mobility	totalitarian	white/blue collar
income ratio		

RECOMMENDED READING

1. The U.S. Department of Commerce, Bureau of the Census, *Statistical Abstract of the United States* and the *Historical Statistics of the United States, Colonial Times to 1970* (http://www.census.gov); and World Bank (annual) *World Development Report,* and *World Development Indicators CD-ROM* provide essential information on the income distributions of the United States and many other societies.

2. *Power and Privilege,* by Gerhard Lenski (NY: McGraw-Hill, 1984). Provides a more detailed analysis of inequality in industrial societies (Chapters 10–12) than is possible in *Human Societies.*

3. *Social Stratification and Inequality,* by Harold Kerbo (NY: McGraw-Hill, 2008); and *The American Class Structure: In an Age of Growing Inequality,* by Dennis Gilbert (Thousand Oaks, CA: Pineforge, 2008). Two very good sources on stratification in the United States from somewhat different points of view.

4. *The Declining Significance of Race: Blacks and Changing American Institutions* (Chicago: University of Chicago Press, 1980); *When Work Disappears: The World of the New Urban Poor* (NY: Knopf, 1996); and *The Truly Disadvantaged: The Inner City, the Underclass, and Public Policy* (Chicago: University of Chicago Press, 1987), all by William Julius Wilson. Three important books, by a noted African American sociologist, on the changing dynamics of race, class, and economics in America.

5. *America in Black and White: One Nation, Indivisible,* by Stephan Thernstrom and Abigail Thernstrom (NY: Simon & Schuster, 1999). A well-written and thoroughly documented analysis of the economic, social, and political progress of African Americans in the United States since 1940. Essential history for those who would like to understand the present.

6. *The Vertical Mosaic,* by John Porter (Toronto: University of Toronto Press, 1965); and *Social Stratification in Canada,* by James Curtis and William Scott, eds. (Scarborough, ON: Prentice-Hall of Canada, 1979). Good sources on stratification in Canada.

7. *Women's Wages and Work in the Twentieth Century,* by James P. Smith and Michael P. Ward (Santa Monica: RAND, 1984). Thoroughgoing and challenging analysis of long-term trends in women's employment and income in the United States.

8. *Did British Capitalism Breed Inequality?* by Jeffrey Williamson (Boston: Allen & Unwin, 1985). A valuable study that supports the thesis that inequality peaked early in the industrial era and has been declining since then.

QUIZ QUESTIONS

Fill-in-the-Blank

1. Because total incomes in industrial societies have steadily increased, competition for income can be characterized as a _____ game.

2. Tracing developments from hunting and gathering through horticulture, agriculture, and industrialization, it is clear that stratification systems have become increasingly _____.

3. If income is equally distributed, the top-earning 20 percent of the population will receive ____ percent of the total income.

4. Race, sex, and ethnicity are examples of _____ characteristics.

5. Recent figures indicate that, on average, women in industrial societies earn about ____ percent of what men earn.

6. Open your book to page 265. Based on the data in Table 12.2, arrange the following societies on the basis of the amount of income inequality in them, starting with the most *un*equal and ending with the most equal: United States, Canada, and Denmark.
(1) _____ (2) _____ (3) _____

True or False

7. There is more income inequality in the typical advanced industrial society today than there was in the typical agrarian.

8. The average income gap between black and white *individuals* has remained basically unchanged over the past forty years or so.

9. Between 1900 and 2005 blue-collar occupations grew faster than white-collar.

10. The gap between rich and poor *societies* has been steadily closing in recent decades.

11. Women in the United States today still earn, on average, less than 50 percent of what men earn.

12. Age and sex differences have always played an important role in societies' divisions of labor and systems of stratification.

13. The income distribution of the United States is more unequal than those of most other industrial societies.

14. Income inequality in the United States is greater today than at any other time in its history.

15. Wealth inequality has steadily increased over the past eighty years in the United States.

16. Low income and poverty are more likely to be permanent statuses in industrial societies than they were in agrarian societies.

17. Women in nonindustrial societies are more likely to hold seats in parliaments than are women in industrial societies.

18. The income gap between employed black and white individuals has been closing in recent decades.

19. If the ratio of top to bottom income is 1.5 in Finland and 2.0 in Canada, there is *more* income inequality in Canada.

20. In recent years, women's incomes, on average, have grown faster than men's.

21. Slightly more than 10 percent of the workforce in the United States is currently employed in farming.

22. The quality of life in industrial societies is actually *worse* than it is in nonindustrial societies.

Multiple Choice

23. As the subsistence technologies of societies have advanced from hunting and gathering through horticulture, agriculture, and industry, systems of stratification have grown more:
    a) unfair
    b) open
    c) unpredictable
    d) closed
    e) complex

24. According to Table 12.1, _____ has more (a total of four) of the fifteen richest individuals in the world than any other.
    a) the United States
    b) the United Kingdom
    c) Canada
    d) Saudi Arabia
    e) the United Arab Emirates

25. Which of the following *ratios* of the incomes of the highest-earning 20 percent to those of the lowest-earning 40 percent (highest 20/lowest 40) would indicate the greatest *inequality*?
    a) 0.20
    b) 0.40
    c) 1.0
    d) 2.0
    e) 3.0

26. Which of the following is true about the trend in *income* inequality in the United States over the past seventy-five years or so?
    a) It decreased, leveled off, and then increased.
    b) It has steadily declined.
    c) It has steadily increased.
    d) It has been remarkably stable.
    e) none of the above

27. The category of occupations that *declined* the most in percentage terms between 1900 and 2005 was:
    a) farmer and farm laborer

    b) upper white-collar
    c) lower white-collar
    d) upper blue-collar
    e) lower blue-collar

28. Which of the following is/are true about differences in income by race in the United States?
    a) The gap between black family income and white family income has closed over the past forty years.
    b) The income gap between white and black women is greater than the gap between white and black men.
    c) The income gap between employed black men and employed white men has remained virtually unchanged over the past sixty years.
    d) all of the above
    e) none of the above

29. Comparing agrarian societies with industrial societies, it appears that:
    a) political inequality is greater in agrarian societies, but economic inequality is greater in industrial societies
    b) both types of inequality tend to be greater in agrarian societies
    c) both types of inequality tend to be greater in industrial societies
    d) economic inequality is greater in agrarian societies, but political inequality is greater in industrial societies
    e) there is little difference in the degree of inequality between these two types of societies

30. Inequality between the sexes in modern industrial societies is:
    a) greater than it has ever been before in human societies
    b) greater than in agrarian societies, but not as pronounced as in more primitive societies
    c) greater than ever before in the political realm, but less than it used to be in the economic
    d) greater than ever before in the economic realm, but less than it used to be in the political
    e) none of the above

31. According to Table 12.4, the median ratio of women to men's income in industrial societies is about:
    a) 52
    b) 63
    c) 66
    d) 78
    e) 89

32. Recruitment and promotion patterns in modern industry resemble those developed earlier in:
    a) the military
    b) penal institutions
    c) British Colonies (e.g., Australia)
    d) lotteries
    e) athletics

33. According to Chapter 12, today the ratio of the highest-earning to the lowest-earning families in the United States is about:
    a) 10 to 1
    b) 100 to 1
    c) 1,000 to 1
    d) 10,000 to 1
    e) 100,000 to 1

34. The most dramatic change in the occupational structure of the United States since 1900 has been:
    a) the decline in farm employment
    b) the increase in blue-collar employment
    c) the decline in white-collar employment
    d) the increase in farm employment
    e) none of the above

35. Since 1940, the percentage of African Americans in middle class occupations has:
    a) increased substantially
    b) remained about the same
    c) decreased substantially
    d) increased until 1970 and then decreased
    e) none of the above

36. One of the most important factors responsible for the continuing gap in the incomes of black and white *families* has been:
    a) the legal barriers still confronting blacks
    b) the growing number of black female-headed households
    c) the rising cost of living in the United States
    d) rising rates of inflation
    e) none of the above

37. One of the most important reasons women continue to earn less than men in the United States is:
    a) there are still laws restricting a woman's right to own property
    b) women continue to face numerous educational barriers
    c) women are concentrated in low-paying jobs
    d) the rising cost of living in the United States
    e) none of the above

38. During the industrial era, the gap between rich and poor *societies* has:
    a) opened and closed in regular cycles
    b) steadily closed
    c) steadily widened
    d) fluctuated randomly
    e) none of the above

39. Overall, the level of inequality in industrial societies is _____ it was in agrarian societies of the past and in most nonindustrial societies today.
    a) considerably higher than
    b) a little bit higher than

c) about the same as
d) a little bit less than
e) considerably less than

Essay/Study Questions

40. What are some of the most important trends in the stratification of industrial societies? How can they be explained?

41. Why is it important to distinguish the *income* of population segments from their income *share*?

42. In what ways is stratification more complex in industrial societies than it was in agrarian?

43. What are some of the most important reasons that political inequality is less in industrial societies than it was in agrarian?

44. Trace the changes in stratification that have occurred as societies changed from hunting and gathering to horticulture, agriculture, and industry.

45. Why is competition for income a positive-sum "game" in industrial societies?

46. Why and how do race and sex continue to affect stratification in advanced industrial societies?

47. What do you think Karl Marx would say if he could see the data on trends in income inequality, wealth ownership, and standards of living presented in Chapter 12?

48. What explains the apparent contradiction between the fact that on the one hand African Americans appear to have made great economic gains in recent decades, and on the other, that nothing has really changed very much, or they may actually have lost ground?

49. What explains the apparent contradiction between the fact that on the one hand women appear to have made great economic gains in recent decades, and on the other, that nothing has really changed very much?

NOTES

[1] It is also important to recognize the fact that the average standard of living of a population is different from the relative equality or inequality of the *distribution* of valued resources in that population. In fact, it is quite possible for the average standard of living to increase dramatically if inequality in the distribution of income or wealth remains the same, or even increases.

[2] Revolutionary socialist societies such as the former Soviet Union and eastern European Communist societies were clear exceptions to this statement. We will discuss these "massive social experiments" in a little more detail in an excursus to Chapter 14.

[3] Estimates of the trend in wealth owned by the top 1 percent of *households* shows a much more volatile up-and-down pattern, with inequality today similar to that in 1922. For example, see Ed-

ward N. Wolff, "Changing Inequality in Wealth," *American Economic Review* 82 (May 1992); and "The Great Wealth Divide: The Growing Gap in the United States Between the Rich and the Rest," *Multinational Monitor* (May 2003).

[4] When reporting changes in family income, they also generally neglect the fact that the *average size* of families declined significantly in this period (e.g., see pages 284–87).

[5] Consider also the high levels of "quality of life" in industrial societies and their contrast with the nonindustrial world (e.g., Table 12.5 on page 277).

[6] Recall the *caveats* in our discussion of the changing occupational structure in Chapter 10 of this *Primer and Guide.*

[7] The comparable figures for white families today are 18.2 and 30.5 percent, respectively.

[8] The disparities between black and white two-parent households are substantially lower. Recent figures show that black married-couple households earn 84 percent of the income of white married-couple households.

[9] Despite unprecedented movement by women into "traditionally male" occupations (e.g., physician, lawyer, engineer), *most* women continue to be employed in traditionally female occupations (e.g., secretary, nurse, elementary school teacher). As the discussion on pages 287–93 and the boxed insert on page 292 indicate, the reasons for persistence of these differences in occupation and earnings are varied and complex.

[10] Don't be confused by the different gender ratios that are presented and discussed in the media and elsewhere—the ratio of hourly wages (which generally shows the smallest gap), the ratio of income for all people with income (which generally shows the largest gap), or the ratio for full-time, full-year workers (which generally shows an intermediate-sized gap). All indicate the same trend of decrease (e.g., see Figure 12.5 on page 274), but since they relate to people with very different involvement in the labor force, one must be careful to compare figures for similarly situated workers/earners.

[11] This is not surprising when you consider the dramatic changes that have occurred in women's education (e.g., see Table 13.4 on page 291).

13

Industrial Societies

Population, the Family, and Leisure

CHAPTER SUMMARY

The chapter opens with a discussion of the key demographic trends in industrial societies: the improvements in health and increased longevity, the declining birthrates, the high rates of immigration into industrial societies, and the growth of urban communities. This is followed by discussion of the changing functions of the family and other changes that industrialization has brought about in the kinship systems of industrial societies. Then, after briefly indicating the most important causes of these changes, the chapter examines the changed and changing roles of women and youth in industrial societies. This is followed by discussion of leisure and the arts and of the growing impact of the mass media, especially television, on the daily life of members of industrial societies. It closes with a brief survey of problems and prospects faced by industrial societies—a topic that is discussed in greater detail in the final chapter—and a broad overview of industrial societies from the perspective of ecological-evolutionary theory.

Falling rates of mortality followed, in turn, by falling rates of fertility—a pattern of change commonly referred to as the "demographic transition" are largely responsible for the revolutionary and unparalleled developments that have occurred in industrial societies. As we noted in Chapter 10, this dramatic shift in birth and death rates is partially responsible for the massive increase in the economic surplus produced in industrial societies (e.g., see pages 219–220). Table 13.1 (page 279) shows the precipitous decline in death rates for selected diseases, and Table 13.2 (page 281) a key consequence of that decline, the current very low levels of fertility in industrial societies.

As the data in Table 13.2 show, the total fertility rates of *almost all* the industrial societies are now *below replacement*.[1] At these rates, if no one moved into them, their populations *would actually shrink substantially* over the next seventy years. But while fertility has been plummeting in industrial societies, it has remained high in much of the Third World. This, together with rapidly dropping mortality, has produced unprecedented rates of population growth in the Third World (e.g., see Table 14.2 on page 304). It is not surprising, therefore, that there has been substantial migration *out* of Third World and *into* advanced industrial societies in recent decades. And, although this helped for a time to alleviate labor shortages (most notably in low-paying and undesirable jobs that native-born citizens didn't want), it has greatly increased the potential for cultural misunderstandings and conflict in advanced industrial societies.

The commingling of people from such different cultural backgrounds and with such different experiences with the technology and social organization of industrial societies has created powerful tensions and explosive situations in many of these societies, especially when they have been combined with persisting high rates of unemployment. In some cases, these tensions have resulted in ethnic violence, and there are signs that they will become more widespread and more serious in the years ahead. It is, thus, important to understand the underlying demographic causes of these tensions and conflicts.

Growth in urban populations in industrial societies has nearly reversed the rural to urban population ratios of agrarian societies.[2] Whereas about 90 percent of the population of agrarian societies lived in rural areas, in advanced industrial societies, more than 75 percent live in *urban* areas.[3] These population dynamics together with the technological and economic changes that have accompanied advancing industrialization have had profound effects on the institution of the family. The technological, ideological, economic, and occupational changes of the industrial era have changed the social roles of men and women and have altered the size, structure, and functioning of the family. Industrial families are generally smaller than those of agrarian and horticultural societies[4]—they are nuclear rather than extended—and they perform many fewer basic *social* functions.

Educational opportunities for women have been vastly expanded in industrial societies.[5] In fact, Table 13.4 on page 291 shows that women now earn the majority of bachelor's degrees in the United States, and nearly half of the doctorate and law degrees.

But perhaps the most dramatic change has been in the role(s) of women in industrial societies. A large and growing majority of women are now in the paid labor force (see Figure 13.1 on page 289),[6] many in managerial positions, and a substantial number are in politics (e.g., see Table 13.5 on page 291). At the same time, there has been an increase in the proportion of households and families that are headed by women—in 1970, 21 percent of households and 11 percent of families were headed by women; in 2006, 30 percent of households and 18 percent of families were female-headed.

A number of factors have contributed to the increase in female employment. Among the most important have been the declines in infant and child mortality (whereas 99 percent of the babies born into advanced industrial societies will live to celebrate their fifteenth birthdays, half or more of the babies born into preindustrial societies died before they reached the age of fifteen); the development of a number of time- and labor-saving household technologies (e.g., hot water heaters, refrigerators, washing machines); the tremendous growth in white-collar occupations and in the service sector of industrial economies; and, to a certain degree, desires for a higher living standard.

Declining mortality contributed to this change in women's roles by fostering a decline in fertility. As we have seen, the birthrates of industrial societies are only about a third of those in agrarian. Table 13.3 (page 285) presents some data on the decline in the number of children born into industrial families. Compare the percentages of marriages formed in 1860 that produced three or fewer children to the percentage of marriages formed in 1925 that produced so few children.[7] This decline reflects not only the improved chances of children surviving but also the increased economic *costs* of raising children in industrial societies.

Declining fertility and the development of labor-saving technology made it *possible* for women, especially married women, to participate more in the paid labor force, but it was the economic "pull" of the increased demand for workers, growing aspirations for a higher standard of living, and the economic "push" of rising costs of living that made this possibility a *reality* for increasing numbers of married women. For, as Figure 13.2 (page 290) suggests, a large number of women, especially married women with children, are "pushed" into and kept in the paid labor force not to *raise* family income, but to *maintain it.*

Furthermore, it is important to recognize that although attitudes about sex roles and work have changed in industrial societies, their change is more a *consequence* than it is a *cause* of changes in the structure and functioning of families in industrial societies. As increasing numbers of women were employed full-time, and as larger numbers of women headed families, they began to raise questions about the pay inequities and occupational barriers they faced. The time demands of full-time employment also put pressure on "traditional" family roles and the "traditional" allocation of household and child-care responsibilities among husbands, wives, and older children.

As we noted in earlier chapters, families and kinship groups once performed *all* the functions now served by courts, police, schools, businesses, armies, welfare agencies, banks, and governments. Today they are primarily units of economic *consumption* and social and psychological supports for their members. As a result they have increasingly become *optional.* In fact, larger numbers of people are choosing not to marry—in 1970, 16 percent of the U.S. population over age eighteen was single (never married); today more than twenty-five percent is. The "traditional" two-parents-with-children family is thus an ever-shrinking proportion of U.S. *households.* In 2006 only about 51 percent of U.S. *households* were married couples, and a mere 23 percent were married couples with children.

Nonetheless, even in the most advanced industrial societies, there is still a division of labor between the sexes in which men spend more time, on average, working for pay, and women spend more time on housework and child care. Taken together with the high levels of employment of women, and women with children, this highlights some of the tensions and stresses currently facing families in advanced industrial societies.

Another development in industrial societies has been the development of a youth subculture.[8] Ironically, this subculture, which exists in part because of the increasing demand for highly educated workers in advanced industrial societies, places a higher value on such things as athletics than it does on learning or preparation for work—this, despite the fact that a *successful* high school athlete's chances of making a living in sports are remote. Not too long ago, the probability of a high school athlete being able to make it to the professional ranks of basketball was 0.0006 (about 6 out of ten thousand) and for football it was 0.001 (one out of a thousand).[9]

Television continues to be a major component of leisure activities, and it is certainly one of the key technologies that have transformed social and political life in industrial societies. A good deal of time and effort has been expended to determine whether or not there is a political bias in the mass media, especially television. But the most obvious bias of television is not political but *visual*; it is biased toward the visually exciting and dramatic, and away from the complicated, subtle, and tedious (e.g., note the photo of people running from the collapsing World Trade Center on page 255). Therefore, important but subtle or complex issues are typically passed over or reduced to simplistic proportions. Television neither seeks out, nor reports well on, issues and stories that have no visual features or that are without clearly perceptible and immediate impact on viewers. As a result, visually exciting stories (spectacular fires, crashes, etc.) crowd out more complicated and less exciting stories that actually may have more long-term impact on, and importance for, citizens and viewers.[10]

Consequently, to the extent that people rely on TV for information and news, they are likely to get a very distorted view of reality. Similarly distorted views may also be fostered by television entertainment. Few people featured in television shows have ordinary or dull jobs, and when they do they were often the subject of considerable humor (see the Kalaski paper recommended below). Moreover, characters on TV with exciting or interesting jobs will generally face more adventure and drama in a single episode than most real incumbents of these jobs face in a career.

The chapter closes with a review of developments that have occurred over the industrial era; it is similar in many ways to the review of developments up through the end of the agrarian era at the end of Chapter 8 (pages 184–86). Although many of these developments are simply continuations of earlier trends (e.g., growing technological productivity, increasing social complexity, increasingly destructive military technology), a few notable ones are reversals of earlier trends (e.g., political and economic inequality, upward mobility). We will consider these long-term trends again in the final chapter of *Human Societies,* where we will also try to make some projections into the future.

IMPORTANT TERMS

extended family	nuclear family	siblings
youth subculture	mass media	propaganda
demographic transition	total fertility rate	mass media
replacement	immigration	emigration
labor force participation	communicable	life expectancy

RECOMMENDED READING

1. The *Statistical Abstract of the U.S.* and *Historical Statistics of the U.S. Colonial Times to 1970,* by U.S. Department of Commerce, Bureau of the Census, provide essential information on households and families in the United States (http://www.census.gov). For more detailed data on families, income, and poverty, see also, Current Population Reports such as: "Income, Poverty, and Health Insurance in the United States: 2006," (http://www.census.gov/prod/2007pubs/p60-233.pdf)

2. See *Population Reference Bureau* reports, (http://www.prb.org/) and *National Vital Statistics Reports* (http://www.cdc.gov/nchs/products/pubs/pubd/nvsr/54/54-pre.htm), for the latest data on disease, birth, death, marriage, and divorce rates.

3. Periodic reports and publications such as: Forbes' *The 100 Most Powerful Women* (http://www.forbes.com/lists/2007/11/biz-07women_The-100-Most-Powerful- Women_Rank.html); *Women of Our World 2005,* and "Taking Stock of Women's Progress," by Lori Ashford, from the *Population Reference Bureau* (http://www.prb.org/); and earlier publications such as: *Women's Figures: An Illustrated Guide to the Economic Progress of Women in America,* by Diana Furchtgott-Roth and Christine Stolba (Washington, DC: American Enterprise Institute, 1999); and *World's Women: Trends and Statistics, 1970–1990,* by the United Nations (NY: United Nations, 1991), are excellent sources of cross-national statistics on women.

4. *Women's Wages and Work in the Twentieth Century,* by James P. Smith and Michael P. Ward (Santa Monica, CA: RAND, 1984). A thorough-going and challenging analysis of long-term trends in women's employment and income in the United States. For periodically updated data on the female/male income ratio for full-time, full-year

workers, see *Women's Earnings as a Percentage of Men's, 1951–2006* (http://www.infoplease.com/ipa/A0193820.html).

5. *The Myth of Family Decline: Understanding Families in a World of Rapid Social Change,* by Edward L. Kain (Lexington, MA: Lexington Books, 1990). Challenging view of families in industrial societies from a comparative-evolutionary perspective.

6. *The Second Sex,* by Simone de Beauvoir (NY: Random House, 1989 [1952]). Classic analysis of the role of women in society. See especially Parts II and VII.

7. *The Mass Media Election,* by Thomas E. Patterson (NY: Praeger, 1980). Provides a fascinating analysis of the role of the mass media in the 1976 presidential election.

8. *The Powers That Be,* by David Halberstam (NY: Dell, 1979). A study of the media and their influence in the United States.

9. "TV's Unreal World of Work," by Robert Kalaski (*American Federationist* 1980). Brief report of a study of the world of work as portrayed, and distorted, by television. A number of years old, but it's not clear that things have changed very much, at least not for the better.

QUIZ QUESTIONS

Fill-in-the-Blank

1. A/an _____ family consists of parents and their unmarried children, whereas a/an _____ family consists of several generations and other relatives.

2. The shift from a near balance of high birth and high death rates to one of low birth and low death rates is called _____.

3. The death rates from _____ have dropped dramatically in industrial societies.

4. Approximately ___ percent of babies born in industrial societies can expect to celebrate their fifteenth birthdays.

5. Whereas the average life expectancy in many advanced agrarian societies was only about ____ years, it is more than ____ years in industrial societies.

6. A TFR of about ___ is required to "replace" parents in the next generation.

7. The average TFR in industrial societies is today about ____.

8. Brothers and sisters are also referred to as _____.

9. Because young people in industrial societies spend so much time together in educa-

tional institutions before they assume adult roles, they have developed a distinctive

_____.

10. About _____ percent of all American women are employed outside the home today.

11. The systems of communication that can reach large numbers of people are referred to collectively as the _____.

12. The most basic underlying force effecting societal change and development in industrial societies has been, and continues to be _____.

13. In the United States today, women earn more _____ degrees than men.

14. Whereas only about ____ percent of the populations of agrarian societies lived in urban areas, ____ percent of the populations of advanced sindustrial societies live in urban areas.

15. Whereas in 1890 only about 6 percent of people aged fourteen to seventeen were enrolled in school, today about _____ percent are enrolled.

True or False

16. The average infant born in an industrial society can expect to live more than seventy years.

17. Although tuberculosis claimed the lives of nearly 200 people per 100,000 population in the U.S. in 1900, it claimed less than 1 per 100,000 population in 2004.

18. According to the data in Table 13.2 (page 281), the total fertility rate in most industrial societies is below the number required for parents to replace themselves.

19. Although the industrial nuclear family is no longer the primary unit of economic *consumption,* it remains the primary unit of economic *production.*

20. More families may have been broken by death in agrarian societies than are broken by divorce in industrial societies today.

21. Three-year old children in the United States spend, on average, ___ hours per week watching television.

22. If the world returned to the technology of the agrarian era, 75 percent or more of the world's current population would have to die.

23. Technological change is no longer the most important underlying force responsible for societal change in industrial societies.

24. The greatest threats facing the biophysical environments of industrial societies today are the feedback effects of prior human activity and technology.

25. Marriages are more likely to be formed for personal reasons in industrial societies than they were in either horticultural or agrarian.

26. According to Figure 13.1, at every age there is a lower proportion of women in the paid labor force in 2005 than there was in 1890, or 1960.

27. Youth cultures have been found in virtually all types of societies.

28. Changes in attitudes and values have been more important causes of changing sex roles in industrial societies than have changes in technology and the economy.

Multiple Choice

29. In order for an industrial population to maintain its size, the "typical" woman in it must have:
    a) 2.00 children
    b) 2.11 children
    c) 2.45 children
    d) 2.60 children
    e) 2.75 children

30. Which of the following is *not* a consequence of advancing industrialization?
    a) growth in urban populations
    b) a decline in the death rates from communicable diseases
    c) declining total fertility rates
    d) increasing consumption of energy and materials
    e) none of the above (all of these are consequences of industrialization)

31. Which of the following was *not* affected by industrialization?
    a) the size of families
    b) the functions of the family
    c) the role of women
    d) the role of youth
    e) none of the above (all of these were affected)

32. The average number of children born to British married couples in 1860 was ____ and in 1925 was ___.
    a) 10 . . . 5
    b) 5 . . . 10
    c) 6 . . . 2
    d) 2 . . . 6
    e) none of the above

33. The most important cause of change in the role of women in industrial societies is/was:
    a) changes in societal attitudes
    b) feminist organizations
    c) technological change

    d) hormonal changes caused by improved nutrition
    e) none of the above

34. In the United States today, about ___ percent of women are in the paid labor force.
    a) 49
    b) 59
    c) 69
    d) 79
    e) 89

35. Which of the following is/are true about the trends in the incomes of families in recent decades?
    a) The average income of all married-couple families increased.
    b) The average income of married-couple families where both spouses work increased substantially.
    c) The average income of married-couple families where only the husband works didn't change very much.
    d) all of the above
    e) none of the above

36. Which of the following is/are true about trends in female labor force participation?
    a) More younger women worked in 1890 than in 2005.
    b) More older women worked in 1890 than in 2005.
    c) More women at every age worked in 2005 than in 1890 or 1960.
    d) More younger women worked in 1960 than in 2005.
    e) More older women worked in 1960 than in 2005.

37. Which of the following developed for the first time in industrial societies?
    a) a youth subculture
    b) broken families
    c) social inequality
    d) sexual inequality
    e) crime and homicide

38. Technological change in industrial societies has:
    a) contributed to mortality declines
    b) reduced the labor needed to maintain families
    c) increased employment opportunities for women
    d) all of the above
    e) none of the above

39. Which of the following is/are true about families in industrial societies?
    a) They remain the basic unit of economic production.
    b) They have gained many new social functions.
    c) They have become more of an option than a necessity.
    d) all of the above
    e) none of the above

40. Which of the following is/are true about education in the United States today.
    a) More women than men now receive bachelors' degrees.

b) Women earn about 49 percent of the doctorates (Ph.Ds).

c) Women earn nearly half of the law and medicine degrees.

d) all of the above

e) none of the above

41. According to the text, if the world were to return to the technology of the agrarian era:
    a) most people would be better off economically
    b) most people would be healthier and would live longer
    c) many of the world's problems would be solved
    d) things wouldn't change very much
    e) none of the above

42. Which of the following is a long-term development in industrial societies?
    a) an increasing division of labor *within* and *among* societies
    b) increasing productivity
    c) an increase in the destructive potential of military technology
    d) an increase in the number and variety of symbol systems
    e) all of the above

Essay/Study Questions

43. What are some of the most basic changes in the functions of the family that have occurred as a result of the Industrial Revolution?

44. What does it mean to say that industrial families are basic economic units of *consumption* but not of *production*? How does this compare to agrarian societies?

45. If, in the near future, technology makes it easily possible for people to reproduce in "test tubes," do you think *families* will become extinct? Why or why not?

46. What are some of the reasons that families in industrial societies have so many fewer children than did families in agrarian societies?

47. Why do you think there continues to be a division of labor between men and women in advanced industrial societies? Do you think the roles of men and women will ever be exactly the same? Would that be a good thing? Why, or why not?

48. How does TV distort our view of society? What kinds of events is television likely to report? ignore?

49. How has industrialization changed the status and role of youth?

50. Arrange the following variables into a model showing their interrelationships in industrial societies. Be sure to include feedback effects and distinguish them from direct effects.
    Birth rates, Death rates, Technological advance, Size and composition of families, Percentage of women in the paid labor force, Occupational structure, Economy, Sex role attitudes, Family division of labor.

51. What are some of the important demographic changes that have occurred in industrial societies? in the world system of societies?

52. Why is migration into industrial societies increasing? Where are these people coming from? What problems are likely to result from this massive influx of people?

53. Explain, if you can, how more women can earn bachelors' degrees than men and get nearly half the doctorates, and yet still earn less income, on average, than men?

NOTES

[1] The single clear exception is Israel, a society that only recently crossed the industrial "threshold." Note that total fertility rate (TFR) is an estimate of the total number of children a "typical" woman will have in a society. As the text discussion of it notes, because some babies will not survive to adulthood or will be unable to reproduce if they do, a TFR of about 2.11 provides "replacement" of the mother *and* the father in the next generation; a TFR lower than this indicates the population will decline (if no one moves into it); a TFR greater than this indicates the population will grow (if no one moves out of it).

[2] This shift in population is largely a product of the increasing productivity of agricultural technology (e.g., see Table 10.1 on page 216).

[3] Although many large urban centers in the United States have lost population in recent decades, there has not been a substantial increase in *rural* population. This is because most of the people who have left urban centers have located in areas adjacent to (suburbs), or within commuting distance of, these urban centers.

[4] They also continue to shrink in size. Between 1960 and 2006 the average size of *families* in the United States declined from 3.7 to 3.1, and the average size of *households* declined from 3.3 to 2.6.

[5] For the stark contrast with women's status in many developing societies, see pages 315–16 in the next chapter of *Human Societies*.

[6] To determine the percentage of women at a given age who are employed in a given year, draw a line vertically from age until it meets the curve for the year and then move to the left until you cross the percentage line—this is the percentage of women this age who are employed in the paid labor force this year. For instance, about 17 percent of women ages 25–34 were employed in 1890, 36 percent in 1960, and about 74 percent in 2005.

[7] 28 percent (9 + 5 + 6 + 8) versus 80 percent (17 + 24 + 25 + 14). Conversely then, 72 percent had more than three children in 1860, while only 20 percent did in 1925.

[8] A subculture is a group that develops an identity, a set of values, and norms that are different from (although not necessarily opposed to) the larger (dominant) culture.

[9] The probability is simply the relative frequency of the numbers of professional and high school athletes—0.0006 = 304/513,000 and 0.001 = 1,232/930,000.

[10] Unlike newspapers and news magazines, television technology does not allow its consumers to "turn the page"; it forces everyone to watch the same stories at the same time. As a result, if it is to maintain its viewers (and this is what generates its advertising revenues), it cannot afford to alienate viewers. It thus ends up trying to find the "lowest common denominator"—stories and programs that appeal to everyone.

14

Industrializing Societies

CHAPTER SUMMARY

This chapter opens with a discussion of the importance of distinguishing between societies that have a tradition of plow agriculture—industrializing agrarian societies—and those that have a tradition of hoe horticulture—industrializing horticultural societies. For a variety of reasons, the economic difficulties facing industrializing horticultural societies are especially severe. They have even less of the infrastructure necessary to support an industrial economy (e.g., good roads, an educated workforce, stable governments), and rely on even fewer exports than for income than do industrializing agrarian societies). But an even more serious barrier is posed by their high rates of population growth (see Table 14.2). Not only does rapid population growth dilute economic gains, but providing sustenance, schooling, and later employment for large and growing numbers of young people challenges the entire institutional fabric of these societies. The inability to cope with this challenge often spawns growing poverty, political repression (e.g., see Table 14.3), political corruption (e.g., see Table 14.4), violent ethnic and political strife, civil wars, and terrorism. It also makes radical ideologies such as Islamic fundamentalism attractive to large numbers of disaffected youth. The chapter closes with a critical examination of the social science explanations that have been offered for the slow and distorted development of industrializing agrarian and horticultural societies—dependency theory, modernization theory, and ecological-evolutionary theory. A discussion of societies that attempted to put revolutionary socialism (see Chapter 11) into practice follows the chapter in an excursus: "Marxist Societies as Natural Experiments." Unfortunately, despite Marx's soaring rhetoric and utopian promises, the results of these experiments were uniformly horrifying.

It is almost impossible to pick up a newspaper without reading about problems in developing societies.[1] Droughts, famines, refugee camps, military coups, civil wars, poverty, epidemics, tribal warfare, accusations of genocide, and the like seem endemic. Why is there so much apparent turmoil and misery in these societies?

One of the key reasons is that these societies are "hybrids" consisting of two very different modes of subsistence side-by-side. In a sense they have a foot in two different worlds: one in preindustrial horticulture or agriculture and the other in industrial. The industrial segment is often so concentrated geographically and so isolated socially that it constitutes, and is sometimes referred to as, an "enclave."

Furthermore, as was the case in each succeeding historical era that preceded it, these societies now face more difficult prospects for survival than they did prior to the industrial era, and more difficult circumstances than those faced by the already industrialized societies. For instance, as they attempt to industrialize, they face a number of *already* industrialized societies; as they experience rapid population growth and high rates of ru-

143

ral-to-urban migration, there is no sparsely settled "New World" to absorb these large and growing "surplus" populations, as there was for industrializing Europe only a few centuries ago. Because the subsistence technology they practiced prior to the industrial revolution continues to play such an important role in determining their present and future prospects, it is important to distinguish *industrializing agrarian* (IA) from *industrializing horticultural* (IH) societies.[2]

Industrializing agrarian societies are found in Mexico, Central and South America, North Africa, and Asia.[3] But, with the exception of Haiti and Papua New Guinea, all of the industrializing horticultural societies are located in a single region on a single continent—Africa below the Sahara Desert.[4] This geographical concentration is largely a result of the unique character of the environment of sub-Saharan Africa. For, although it is very conducive to horticulture, it has been highly resistant to agriculture. Not only is the soil of the tropical rain forest generally unsuitable for plow cultivation, but a number of indigenous diseases have made it difficult to domesticate and raise animals to pull plows.[5] It was thus virtually impossible for agriculture to develop there, and as a result, most societies of sub-Saharan Africa maintained their horticultural mode of subsistence long into the industrial era.

Although their rates of economic growth (GDP) indicate substantial economic advancement for all three types of societies over the past four decades (see Table 14.2 on page 304)—industrial societies grew, on average, 3.7 percent per year, industrializing agrarian 4.5 percent, and industrializing horticultural 3.1 percent—their *per capita* rates tell a very different, and more discouraging story.

In *per capita* terms, the industrializing agrarian societies grew at a rate of 2.4 percent, somewhat slower than the 2.9 percent growth rate of industrial societies, and industrializing horticultural societies barely grew at all, 0.3 percent.[6] The contrast between the total and *per capita* rates of economic growth clearly reveals the role that population growth has played in *undermining* or diluting economic development in industrializing societies, especially those with a horticultural heritage.

As the second row of the table shows, over this time period the populations of industrializing horticultural societies grew, on average, 2.6 percent per year, and those of industrializing agrarian and industrialized grew at rates of 2.1 and 0.8 percent respectively. These may seem to be slow rates of growth and small differences, but at these rates the populations of industrial societies would double in about eighty-seven years,[7] and those of industrializing agrarian and industrializing horticultural societies would double in thirty-three and twenty-seven years, respectively.[8] Thus, in eighty-seven years the populations of industrial societies would be *twice* what they are today, but those of industrializing agrarian societies would be more than *six times,* and industrializing horticultural societies would be more than *nine times,* their current size![9] Clearly such high, and unprecedented, rates of population growth cannot be sustained in industrializing societies; if nothing else intervenes, famines, epidemics, and wars spurred by these high growth rates will act as "natural" brakes.

High rates of population growth constitute a tremendous burden on the educational system, politics, health care, urban communities, and other institutions and resources of these societies. They have also contributed to declines in per capita food production in many industrializing societies, making them even more dependent on the developed world for their sustenance.

But some of the impact of population growth can be more subtle and long-term. For instance, the cumulative effects of such growth can negatively affect the environment. In fact, scientists have noted that the Sahara desert has been progressively moving south in recent decades largely as a result of overgrazing and over intensive use of the land—people stripping the land of trees and shrubbery for use as firewood and building material. Once all such greenery is gone, the natural rain cycle is broken and this creates more desert.[10] Thus, although droughts may be natural phenomena, their frequency and magnitude can, and have been, influenced by human activities.

Viewed in a broader historical perspective, population trends in industrializing societies indicate that industrializing horticultural societies are in an early stage, industrializing agrarian societies are in a later stage, and industrial societies are in the final stage of the "demographic transition." As a result, until very recently, the rate of population growth was actually *increasing* in industrializing horticultural societies, and it was *decreasing* substantially in industrializing agrarian societies. The "good news" is that population growth rates have been declining in recent years, and if development continues, mortality declines can be expected to (eventually) produce substantial declines in fertility and decreasing rates of population growth in industrializing horticultural societies. The "bad news" is that their populations will have grown substantially before they turn this demographic corner. Even if their fertility rates drop quite rapidly, their populations can be expected to grow for decades to come given their current "momentum."[11]

Ironically, since the precipitous drop in mortality in industrializing societies is largely a result of public health, medical, and food assistance from advanced industrial societies, many of the problems facing industrializing horticultural societies may be, at least in part, a consequence of the well-intentioned *help* they have received from more advanced societies.

Industrializing societies have also been pushed to occupy relatively specialized roles in the world economy by the *existence* of already industrialized societies. Because industrial societies already dominate manufacturing and financial services, and are in continuous need of raw materials to support manufacturing, the economies of industrializing societies have been largely structured around the export of raw materials. In fact, in many cases they have sacrificed self-sufficiency to produce cash crops for export, and many have become highly dependent on the export of one or a very few commodities (see Table 14.1 on page 303).

As a consequence, their economies are highly volatile and sensitive to world supplies of a given commodity (e.g. petroleum, cocoa, coffee, cotton). If the price of their exported commodity gets too high, importers will seek substitutes or replacements. In such cases the industrializing societies can be left with high debts, having borrowed money to finance production of that commodity, and with little or no money from exports to pay them.

The hybrid and economically unbalanced nature of these societies has added new cleavages and tensions to them. In the industrializing agrarian societies, there are powerful landowners who have traditionally dominated these societies and who are often the dominant figures in the production of export commodities, and there are peasants who are trying to get, or to hold on to, land. The industrializing horticultural societies are fractured by tribal, ethnic, religious, and linguistic differences (often deliberately fostered and inflamed by colonial powers to enable them to "divide and rule" these societies). In both types of societies, there are also rifts between the poor, the illiterate, the rural, and the well-educated, well-paid professionals in the industrial enclave of the urban industrial economy.

These cleavages, contradictions, and general poverty have made industrializing societies highly receptive to revolutionary ideologies, "millenarian" movements, radical fundamentalism, and, more recently, terrorism. Tensions and conflicts are likely to be most intense if one of the ethnic or religious groups is identified with, and participates in, industrialization and modernization (or "westernization"), and others are excluded or oppose it for religious or cultural reasons.

For some time, Marx's argument that history is on the side of the powerless has had tremendous appeal for both the western-educated intellectual elites and the peasantry in these societies, but more recently there have been backlashes against western ideas, and a variety of ethnic, nationalist, religious, and fundamentalist movements have arisen to oppose modernization. Most recently, it has been Islamic fundamentalism.

Poverty, low levels of literacy and school enrollments, limited development of mass media of communication, and regional, ethnic, and religious divisions have also made it difficult for democratic forms of government to flourish in industrializing societies. Although industrializing agrarian, and more recently industrializing horticultural societies, have been rapidly adopting multiparty democratic *forms* of government, it remains to be seen how well and how long they will be able to sustain them. Moreover, the outward similarities in their *form* of government may mask very real differences in the levels of liberty and freedom afforded to their citizens. Compare, for example, the strikingly different levels of political rights and civil liberties enjoyed by citizens in the different types of societies shown in Table 14.3 (page 308). On a scale where "7" indicates high levels of freedom and liberty, and "1" indicates little or none, industrial societies average (median) 7.0, and industrializing agrarian and industrializing horticultural societies average 5.0 and 4.0, respectively.[12]

In addition to being more oppressive and stratified politically, there also appears to be more income inequality in industrializing societies. Although one should not put too much confidence in the measures of the income distributions reported for developing countries, the most reliable figures available, which are reported in Table 14.5 (page 311), indicate that the highest-earning 20 percent of households in industrial societies claim only 41.3 percent of the total income, those in industrializing agrarian claim 52.8 percent, and those in industrializing horticultural 48.6 percent. The ratio of income share of the top to the lowest-earning 20 percent of households is 5.4 in industrial but is more than 13 in industrializing agrarian, and nearly 8 in industrializing horticultural societies.[13]

Despite these higher inequality ratios in the industrializing societies, however, the data also show that, because of their greater economic productivity, the *incomes* of *both* the richest and poorest advanced industrial households are actually substantially higher than those of the corresponding households in industrializing societies. And, not surprisingly, the "quality of life" in these societies falls in the same rank order as development and income. Whereas industrial societies achieved an average score of 0.95 (see Table 12.5 on page 277), industrializing agrarian attained only 0.76 and industrializing horticultural a dismal 0.42 (see Table 14.6 on page 314).

Finally, as we noted at the end of Chapter 12 (pages 276–77), global inequality has increased in the industrial era, and recent data indicate that this trend continues. For, although inequality within and among industrial societies has declined, the gap between them and industrializing societies has grown, as has the gap between industrializing agrarian and industrializing horticultural societies. In fact, although economic growth and birthrate declines in industrializing agrarian societies have dramatically slowed the growth in the gap between them and the already industrial societies, the explosive population growth in industrializing horticultural societies has left them even further behind. Population growth certainly is not the *only* problem facing these societies, but it is one of the most serious, and it also tends to make many of the other problems and challenges they face even more difficult.[14]

The final unit of this chapter takes a critical look at two theoretical traditions that have been used to explain the problems of the Third World, and it compares them to ecological-evolutionary theory. Modernization theory emphasizes internal causes (e.g., inappropriate values, lack of institutional infrastructure), and dependency theory emphasizes external causes (e.g., trade patterns, level of foreign investment). Despite the insights generated by these alternative theoretical views, they are judged to provide weaker explanations than that provided by ecological-evolutionary theory (EET), in part because of their virtually exclusive emphasis on *either* internal or external factors, rather than both, and because neither recognizes (or anticipates) the critical role played by rapid population growth in undermining economic advance in industrializing societies.

In the excursus we argue that the wholesale social and economic changes that revolutionary-socialist leaders attempted to implement in Russia, eastern-Europe, China, and elsewhere, constitute massive social experiments. Unfortunately, the results of those experiments were brutality, oppression, imprisonment, and death on a scale unparalleled in history. In fact, R. J. Rummel estimates that, excluding combatant casualties in war, revolutionary-socialist governments may have caused the deaths of as many as 148 million people in the 20th century.

Perhaps the most important lesson that can be drawn from this, and a comparison of it, with the relatively successful, limited, pragmatic reforms of the western "democracies" is that *people should be distrustful of social theorists and politicians who promise too much.*

IMPORTANT TERMS

hybrid	modernization	Third World
rate of natural increase	vicious circle	shanty town
tribalism	colonialism	selective diffusion
modernization theory	dependency theory	world system theory
millenarian	traditional/modern attitudes	

RECOMMENDED READING

1. *The World Development Report* and *World Development Indicators CD-ROM,* published annually by the World Bank; the CIA *World Factbook* (http://www.cia.gov/cia/publications/factbook/); The *Population Reference Bureau* (http://www.prb.org); and *The World Almanac and Book of Facts* (NY: World Almanac Books), which is available in inexpensive paperback in bookstores and supermarkets; all contain a wealth of data on industrial and developing societies.

2. Major national newspapers (e.g., *New York Times, Wall Street Journal, Washington Post)* and major newsmagazines (e.g., *The Economist, U.S. News & World Report, Newsweek, Time*) frequently report in-depth background stories on industrializing societies that are essential reading if one hopes to keep up with current developments in these societies.

3. *Inside the Third World: The Anatomy of Poverty,* by Paul Harrison (Sussex: Harvester Press, 1980). Excellent discussion of the Third World and the problems confronting it.

4. *The Process of Economic Growth,* by W. W. Rostow (NY: Norton, 1962). Classic statement of modernization theory.

5. *Becoming Modern: Individual Change in Six Developing Countries,* by Alex Inkeles and David Smith (Cambridge, MA: Harvard University Press, 1974). Major study of the social psychological correlates of modernization.

6. *Capitalism and Underdevelopment in Latin America,* by André Gunder Frank (NY: Monthly Review Press, 1969); and *Economic Development of Latin America: Historical Background and Contemporary Problems,* by Celso Furtado (NY: Cambridge University Press, 1976). Classic statements of dependency theory.

7. *The Modern World-System,* by Immanuel Wallerstein (New York: Academic Press, 1974). Original statement of world-system theory.

8. *Social Change in the Twentieth Century* (NY: Harcourt, Brace, Jovanovich, 1977) and *Social Change in the Modern Era* (NY: Harcourt, Brace, Jovanovich, 1986), both by Daniel Chirot. Developing explanation of world-system change, written from a revisionist world system/dependency theory perspective.

9. "Trajectories of Development," by Gerhard Lenski and Patrick Nolan, *Social Forces* 63 (1984): 1–23; "Trajectories of Development: A Further Test," by Gerhard Lenski and Patrick Nolan, *Social Forces* 64 (1986): 794–95; "Techno-economic Heritage, Patterns of Development, and the Advantage of Backwardness," by Patrick Nolan and Gerhard Lenski, *Social Forces* 64 (1985): 341–358; Gerhard Lenski, and Patrick Nolan, "Trajectories of Development Among Third World Societies," pp. 187–201 in Gerhard Lenski, *Ecological-Evolutionary Theory: Principles and Applications* (Boulder, CO: Paradigm Publishers, 2005); and Patrick Nolan, "Ecological Evolutionary Theory: A Reanalysis and Reassessment of Lenski's Theory for the 21st Century," *Sociological Theory* 22 (2004): 328–37. These studies show how differences in the techno-economic heritages of industrializing societies continue to influence their patterns and prospects of development.

10. "Status in the World Economy and National Structure and Development," *International Journal of Comparative Sociology* 24 (1983): 109–120; and "World System Status, Techno-economic Heritage, and Fertility," *Sociological Focus* 21 (1988): 9–33, both by Patrick Nolan. Two empirical comparisons of world system/dependency and ecological-evolutionary theories.

11. "A Standardized Cross-National Comparison of Incomes," *Sociological Quarterly* 33 (1992): 599–609, by Patrick Nolan; and "International Stratification and Inequality 1960–1980," *International Journal of Contemporary Sociology* 25 (1988): 105–123, by William Breedlove and Patrick Nolan. Two studies of international stratification.

12. *The Tropics and Economic Development: A Provocative Inquiry into the Poverty of Nations,* by Andrew Karmarck (Baltimore, MD: Johns Hopkins, 1976). Excellent brief survey of the many problems—climate, soil, health—confronting industrializing horticultural societies.

13. *Plagues and Peoples,* by William McNeill (Garden City, NY: Anchor, 1976). A comprehensive examination of the interrelationships between disease and the development of human societies. Although it has relevance for *all* human societies, parts of it specifically address Africa and African societies.

14. *Things Fall Apart,* by Chinua Achebe (NY: Fawcett Crest, 1983 [1959]). A novel depicting life in a small (Nigerian) Ibo society just prior to and during its first contact with the British, by one of Nigeria's preeminent authors.

On Marxist Societies as Natural Experiments

15. *Marx & Engels: Basic Writings,* edited by Lewis Feuer (NY: Anchor, 1959); and *The Marx-Engels Reader,* edited by Robert C. Tucker (NY: Norton, 1978). Two very good collections of the writings of Marx and Engels.

16. *Death by Government,* by R. J. Rummel (Edison, NJ: Transaction, 1997). Mind-numbing statistics on "democide," (murder by government).

17. *The Ruling Class,* by Gaetano Mosca (NY: McGraw-Hill, 1939); and *Political Parties: A Sociological Study of the Oligarchical Tendencies of Modern Democracy,* by Robert Michels (Glencoe, IL: Free Press, 1958). Two classic critiques of revolutionary socialism and the utopian predictions of revolutionary socialists.

18. *The New Class: An Analysis of the Communist System,* by Milovan Djilas (NY: Praeger, 1957); and *The Intellectuals on the Road to Class Power: A Sociological Study of the Role of the Intelligentsia in Socialism,* by George Konrád and Ivan Szelényi (NY: Harcourt, Brace, Jovanovich, 1979). Excellent analyses of the centralization of power and of the political and economic roles played by intellectuals in revolutionary-socialist societies.

19. *Political Pilgrims: Travels of Western Intellectuals to the Soviet Union, China, and Cuba, 1928–1978,* by Paul Hollander (NY: Harper & Row, 1981). Scathing critique of how the desire of many western intellectuals to believe that revolutionary-socialism could create problem- and conflict-free societies blinded them to the serious shortcomings of revolutionary-socialist societies.

20. *The Black Book of Communism: Crimes, Terror, Repression,* Stephane Courtois, et al. (Cambridge, MA: Harvard University Press, 1999). This comprehensive volume, written by former Marxists who are area experts, details and documents the terrible human cost of revolutionary Marxism in Asia, Africa, Eastern Europe, and Central and South America.

21. *Reflections on a Ravaged Century* (NY: Norton, 2001). An eminent historian looks back at the horrors inflicted on humanity in the twentieth century by the "big ideas" of Fascism, Naziism, and Communism.

21. *The Harvest of Sorrow: Soviet Collectivization and the Terror-Famine,* by Robert Conquest (NY: Oxford University Press, 1986). An acclaimed historian documents Stalin's use of famine as a weapon of political terror.

22. *Hungry Ghosts: Mao's Secret Famine,* by Jasper Becker (NY: Free Press, 1996). A horrifying account of the human toll of Mao's "Great Leap Forward."

QUIZ QUESTIONS

Fill-in-the-Blank

1. Ecological-evolutionary theory classifies nonindustrial societies on the basis of their
   _____.

2. Name two industrializing agrarian societies:
   1. _____ 2. _____

3. Name two industrializing horticultural societies:
   1. _____ 2. _____

4. Technological change that harnesses greater amounts of nonliving forms of energy to
   do work is called _____, whereas the changes in attitudes and values that
   accompany and accommodate this technological change is called _____.

5. Most industrializing horticultural societies are located in _____.

6. Between 1961 and 2006, the populations of industrializing agrarian societies were
   growing at about _____ percent per year.

7. Between 1961 and 2006, the populations of industrializing horticultural societies
   were growing at about _____ percent per year.

8. The two societies with the largest populations in the world today are: (1)
   _____ and (2) _____.

9. These two societies are both classified as: _____.

10. Approximately ___ percent of the economic growth in industrializing horticultural
    societies between 1961 and 2006 was consumed by population growth.

11. Order the following types of societies in terms of their political rights and civil liber-
    ties by average size of their populations (*lowest* to *highest*): industrial, industrializing
    agrarian, and industrializing horticultural.
    (1) _____, (2) _____, and (3) _____

12. Order the following types of societies in terms of their levels of economic and tech-
    nological development (from *lowest* to *highest*): industrial, industrializing agrarian,
    and industrializing horticultural.
    (1) _____, (2) _____, and (3) _____

13. Order the following types of societies in terms of their average rate of growth of *per cap-
    ita* GDP (from *lowest* to *highest*): industrial, industrializing agrarian, and industrializing
    horticultural.
    (1) _____, (2) _____, and (3) _____

14. Order the following types of societies in terms of income *inequality* (from *lowest* to *highest*): industrial, industrializing agrarian, and industrializing horticultural.
(1) _____, (2) _____, and (3) _____

15. Order the following types of societies in terms of their average "quality of life" and average income (from *lowest* to *highest*): industrial, industrializing agrarian, and industrializing horticultural.
(1) _____, (2) _____, and (3) _____

True or False

16. Today, more people live in industrializing agrarian societies than in any other type of society.

17. Papua New Guinea, Rwanda, and Somalia are industrializing agrarian societies.

18. Mexico, China, and Egypt are industrializing horticultural societies.

19. In recent decades the populations of industrializing horticultural societies have grown about as fast, or faster, than their economies.

20. Industrial societies often can sell their products more cheaply in industrializing societies than the industries of industrializing societies can produce them.

21. Most of the industrializing horticultural societies in the world today are in Asia and South America.

22. Industrial societies have the "richest rich" and the "richest poor" in the world today.

23. There is evidence that slavery is being practiced today in some industrializing societies.

24. Tribalism and tribal conflict are more of a problem in industrializing agrarian than they are in industrializing horticultural societies.

25. The crude birthrates of industrializing horticultural societies have risen dramatically over the past two decades.

26. Women in industrializing societies generally have lower status and fewer rights than do women in industrial societies.

Multiple Choice

27. An industrializing agrarian society:
    a) uses industrial technology to produce agricultural products
    b) until quite recently depended on horticulture for its subsistence
    c) is a hybrid of industrial and agrarian technologies
    d) has not yet developed or adopted the plow
    e) none of the above

28. Rapid population growth in industrializing horticultural societies:
    a) decreases the costs of education
    b) stimulates economic demand for luxury items
    c) has eroded much of their economic growth
    d) all of the above
    e) none of the above

29. More than half of the world's population today lives in:
    a) industrial societies
    b) industrializing agrarian societies
    c) industrializing horticultural societies
    d) industrializing hunting and gathering societies
    e) none of the above

30. Which of the following types of societies currently has the *fastest* rate of population growth?
    a) industrial
    b) industrializing agrarian
    c) industrializing horticultural

31. Which of the following types of societies currently has the *slowest* rate of population growth?
    a) industrial
    b) industrializing agrarian
    c) industrializing horticultural

32. The major exports of industrializing societies often are:
    a) raw materials
    b) manufactured goods
    c) services
    d) electronics
    e) luxury goods

33. The population of China is notable for:
    a) its rapidly decreasing rate of population growth in recent decades
    b) the dramatic increase in its birthrate
    c) the large proportion of its population that lives in urban areas
    d) all of the above
    e) none of the above

34. Most of the industrializing horticultural societies in the world today are found in:
    a) Africa
    b) South America
    c) Central America
    d) Southeast Asia
    e) the Middle East

35. The average rate of population growth in industrializing horticultural societies is:
    a) between 1 and 2 percent
    b) between 2 and 3 percent
    c) between 3 and 4 percent

d) between 4 and 5 percent

e) more than 5 percent

36. Dependency, modernization and ecological-evolutionary theory all share one important feature—each is trying to explain why Third World countries are:
    a) so committed to their religious ideologies
    b) plagued by constant warfare
    c) so unstable politically
    d) troubled by internal tribal conflicts
    e) developing so slowly

37. The theory that argued that inappropriate ("traditional") values and attitudes were a major problem confronting developing societies was called _____ theory.
    a) world system
    b) dependency
    c) ecological-evolutionary
    d) modernization
    e) none of the above

38. Dependency theory:
    a) holds industrial societies responsible for most Third World problems
    b) is a modified version of Marx's theory
    c) was originally developed by Latin American scholars
    d) all of the above
    e) none of the above

39. The greatest deficiency of *both* modernization theory and dependency theory is their failure to recognize:
    a) that capitalist investment can solve most of the problems of Third World nations
    b) the importance of population growth
    c) the importance of ideology
    d) the importance of being earnest
    e) none of the above

40. What was the most important reason that plow agriculture did not emerge in sub-Saharan Africa?
    a) biophysical and environmental barriers
    b) cultural backwardness
    c) European colonization
    d) the absence of horticulture
    e) none of the above

41. Which of the following distinguish(es) the circumstances confronting industrializing societies today from those confronting societies industrializing in the eighteenth and nineteenth centuries?
    a) Fully industrialized societies exist.
    b) The rates of population growth in industrializing societies are much greater today.
    c) There is no sparsely populated, resource-rich "frontier" to be settled.

d) All of the above
e) None of the above

Essay/Study Questions

42. What is the difference between *industrialization* and *modernization*?

43. What does a comparison of rates of economic growth to per capita rates of economic growth suggest about the reasons for slow development in contemporary industrializing societies?

44. Draw a sketch of the "demographic transition" showing where you would place industrial, industrializing agrarian, and industrializing horticultural societies.

45. Why would Marx's theory of social and economic development be appealing to members of industrializing agrarian societies?

46. How does dependence on a few (or even a single) commodity negatively affect the economies of industrializing societies?

47. Discuss some of the linkages between industrialization, westernization, fundamentalism, and terrorism in industrializing societies in the world today.

48. Why would you expect industrializing agrarian societies to be better able than industrializing horticultural societies to cope with, and adjust to, industrialization?

49. Why is it wrong to think that the key problem confronting theories of development is to explain why conditions in industrializing agrarian and industrializing horticultural societies have *worsened* in the industrial era?

50. Various attempts have been made to explain the problems of Third World societies. What is the basic explanation offered by: (1) dependency theory, (2) modernization theory, and (3) ecological-evolutionary theory?

51. According to dependency theory, virtually all of the problems of industrializing societies are a result of their contact and trade with industrial societies. Do you agree? Why or why not?

52. Why is there no description of "industrializing hunting and gathering" or "industrializing fishing" societies in Chapter 14?

53. Why is it too simplistic to view the periodic crises in industrializing societies (e.g., droughts, famines, outbreaks of epidemic disease) simply as "natural" disasters?

54. How does political corruption affect the development of industrializing societies?

55. If we view Marxist societies as social "experiments," what are their key results? What can we learn from them?

noTE/

¹ These societies are sometimes referred to as "Third World" societies, but in the original system of categories developed decades ago, "Third World" was a *residual* category. Every society that was not one of the western "democracies" (First World), or eastern European or former Soviet Union (Second World), was, by default, Third World. One attempt to reduce the tremendous heterogeneity of this category has been to distinguish developing societies (Third World) from non-developing societies (Fourth World). In line with ecological-evolutionary theory, however, we prefer to categorize them by their technological heritages.

² It may be overly optimistic to call them "industrializing." All we wish to do by this designation is to distinguish them from horticultural and agrarian societies prior to the industrial era—these are not living "fossils" of traditional societies frozen in time—and to call attention to the fact that they are feeling the impact of industrial societies and the industrial sectors of their own economies.

³ The thirty-nine societies classified as industrializing agrarian are listed in a footnote on page 302.

⁴ This is why they are often referred to collectively as "sub-Saharan." The twenty-nine societies classified as industrializing horticultural are listed in a footnote on page 302.

⁵ See the excursus at the end of Chapter 6 (pages 135–136) for a more detailed discussion of these issues.

⁶ Even more striking is the fact that between 1970 and 1995 the rate was actually *negative* for industrializing horticultural societies (–0.1), indicating that, for this period, their populations actually grew faster than their economies. This would mean that rather than being positive-sum, or zero-sum, income changes were *negative*-sum for this time period. In fact, at the end of this twenty-six year period, their economies were 77 percent smaller in per capita terms!

⁷ The sixteen most advanced industrial societies grew an average of 0.63 percent annually from 1961 to 2006. At that rate it would take 111 years for their populations to double.

⁸ The approximate time of doubling can be obtained by dividing the rate of increase into the number seventy (e.g., 70/0.8 = 87.5 years, 70/2.1 = 33.3 years, 70/2.6 = 26.9 years).

⁹ With no migration, the *median* populations of advanced industrial, industrializing agrarian, and industrializing horticultural would be approximately 36, 231, and 204 million respectively.

¹⁰ As we noted in Chapter 6, population growth can easily trigger a "positive feedback" cycle in which a shortage of resources encourages people to intensify their collection of existing resources, which, in turn, reduces the supply of these resources further. If stripping the land of trees upsets the rain cycle, it reduces the dwindling supply of natural resources even more, forcing even greater intensification.

¹¹ This is because even if families *immediately* reduce the number of children they have, past high rates of fertility have already produced a large number of young girls who will grow into women and who will have their own children in the near future.

¹² Please note that, for ease of discussion, we have reversed the coding of the original data so that a high score indicates "more" freedom and liberty.

¹³ To avoid confusion, note that this is a slightly different comparison and ratio—the top 20 to bottom 20—than that made earlier—the top 20 to bottom 40 (e.g., Table 12.2 on page 265).

¹⁴ Among the other problems confronting industrializing societies are bureaucratic waste; mismanagement of resources; political corruption (akin to the "proprietary theory of the state"); tribal, linguistic, ethnic, and religious divisions; wars, civil wars, and a large governmental appetite for

military hardware. Recall, however, that Thomas Malthus warned that uncontrolled population growth triggers it own controls—wars, famines, and pestilence.

15

Retrospect and Prospect

CHAPTER SUMMARY

Looking back over our now completed survey of human societies, this chapter addresses the question of whether technological advance has been truly beneficial for our species when judged in terms of its impact on such basic human concerns as freedom, justice, and happiness. After summing up the results of this evaluation, concern shifts to the future. The prospects for population, natural resources, the biophysical environment, technology, ideology, polity, economy, and the world system of societies are examined in some detail. The chapter closes with the prospects for freedom, justice, and happiness.

Having completed our survey of the major types of human societies, we are now in a position to stand back and reflect upon some of the trends in their development, and to try to project existing trends into the future. In the process we can consider some of the less easily quantifiable and more abstract features of human societies.

Although it was relatively easy to document the impact of technological change on such material things as societal complexity, economic inequality, urbanization of population, and life expectancy, it is much more difficult to evaluate its impact on the *quality of life* in societies. It is also harder to be objective, because to *evaluate* requires the application of values. Nonetheless, given their importance and their (almost) universal valuation, it is worth the effort to try to evaluate the consequences of past technological advance for the "higher goals" of humanity—happiness, justice, and freedom—and to try to foresee the consequences of future technological and social change for them.

Despite the fact that attempting to predict the future is a hazardous task, there are some things that we can predict with more confidence than others. For instance, we are generally better able to predict future *problems* than we are to predict future *solutions* to problems and future technological breakthroughs. This is because, in many cases, the seeds of future problems are already planted, whereas possible solutions, and future technological innovations often cannot even be guessed at. The quality of our predictions also depends on the degree to which they are rooted in well-tested theories and long-term human experience. In order to anticipate future levels of human happiness, freedom, and justice, we should therefore first consider past trends in them, and the factors that have shaped those trends.

To evaluate past trends properly, we must distinguish the consequences of technological advance for *elites* from their consequences for the *average members* of societies; as we have noted at several points in our discussion of the various types of societies humans have lived in, technology and technological advance can mean very different things for these two segments of a society's population. This is especially true for the higher goals. Although they have generally increased for elites in *every* technological era, the long-term trends in freedom, justice, and happiness have shown a markedly *curvilinear* trend for the average member of society.[1] They steadily worsened for the average member of society following the adoption of horticulture, but then became somewhat more favorable following the advent of industrialization. This can be seen in Figure 15.1 (page 326), which displays the trends in freedom. It shows that technological advance from hunting and gathering through advanced agriculture produced *declines* in freedom; however, following the industrial revolution, further technological and economic advance produced *increases* in freedom.

Similar patterns of relationship could be shown for happiness and justice. For example, the levels of self-reported happiness parallel the levels of industrial development in these regions of the world. Furthermore, if one evaluates justice in terms of the connection between effort, ability, and social rewards, and if one considers the relative harshness of punishment in preindustrial societies, justice, too, probably reached its lowest point at the agrarian, or perhaps very early industrial, level of technological development.

Thus the levels of human "higher goals" reached their lowest point for the average person in either advanced agrarian or the very early stages of industrial societies. Afterward they rose with further economic and technological advances. The fact that this trend reversed itself over time should caution us not to equate or confuse technological advance with "progress," or to assume that future technological and social changes will *necessarily* produce further improvements in societal levels of happiness, justice, or freedom. If the trend changed direction once, it can change direction again.

This is especially evident if one considers the role that population has played in these trends and if one takes into account projections of world population growth into the next century. Many of the material gains and reversals of trends that occurred in industrial societies are a result of the fact that technological and economic productivity in industrial societies has grown so much faster than population.[2] The difference in these growth rates is what has produced the tremendous increase in the economic surplus of industrial societies, and it is the increase in economic surpluses that has made increasing levels of material wealth and increasing freedom and happiness *possible* in them.[3]

Yet, despite the continuing low rates of population growth in industrial societies, the world's population continues to grow, and the great bulk of its growth is in very poor Third World societies (e.g., see Figure 15.2 on page 331). For, as we saw in Chapter 14, although they have been falling, population growth rates in the poorest Third World societies are still quite high. Since together these societies comprise the majority of the world's population, this growth will not only put a tremendous burden on the development and resources of *these* societies, but in all likelihood it will continue to fuel massive legal and illegal immigration into the more developed societies, and it will place increasing demands and stresses on the world's biophysical environment.

Images of the stark contrasts between the wealthiest and the poorest societies beamed around the globe on television and computer screens will also, in all likelihood, continue to fuel radical ideologies and movements that promise to ameliorate or reverse these "unjust" differences. And continued political violence and terrorism can be expected.

Environmental problems and damage are also especially likely in the Third World, since, in their poverty and quest for rapid development, industrializing societies are less willing and less able to protect their environments.[4] "Global warming," whether largely natural or caused by humans, may be expected to impact future economic and agricultural productivity, and some see signs that world energy production will not be able to keep pace with world energy demand in the near future, in large measure because of the economic gains being achieved by the large populations of China and India.

One way or another, then, the world economy will have to bear the costs of the population and resource problems of the industrializing world.

Although the prospects for technology's race against world population growth are not completely bleak—in fact, there are some signs of progress—it is important to keep in mind, when attempting to anticipate the future, that the people confronting these issues *will be people just like us.* We should neither demonize nor deify them. In the past, people and societies have generally ignored problems until they were *forced* to confront them.[5] We too, have this capacity. We can ignore these problems until it is too late, or we can hope for unanticipated technological breakthroughs that will solve them. One thing is for sure though: this is not simply an exercise in idle speculation. Most of you will live through this period, and by the time you are ready to retire, in the 2050s, or 2060s, you will know the *denouement* of this story.

IMPORTANT TERMS

higher goals	progress	greenhouse effect
nuclear fission	recombinant DNA	energy efficiency
liberation theology	Gross World Product	*denouement*
energy efficiency	monotonic	biological diversity

RECOMMENDED READING

1. *The Ruling Class,* by Gaetano Mosca (NY: McGraw-Hill, 1939). Chapter 11, sections 3 and 4 provide a classic model of social forecasting in which the forecast is clearly and explicitly grounded in theory.

2. *An Inquiry into the Human Prospect,* by Robert Heilbroner (NY: Norton, 1991). A fascinating view of the future that challenges our normal tendencies toward optimism. This view of the future, like Mosca's, is clearly and explicitly grounded in theory (or, more accurately, it rests on the foundation of some clearly stated and reasonable assumptions).

3. *Building a Sustainable Society,* by Lester Brown (NY: Norton, 1981). This is something of an updated version of Brown's earlier book, *In the Human Interest* (NY: Norton, 1974).

4. *State of the World,* by Lester Brown, and *Vital Signs: The Trends That Are Shaping Our Future,* by Lester Brown, et al. Two annual publications by the Worldwatch Institute that present data, trends, and analyses concerning the condition of the planet and its likely prospects.

5. *The Resourceful Earth: A Response to Global 2000,* by Julian Simon and H. Kahn (NY: Basil Blackwell, 1984). A perspective on population growth very different from that articulated by Brown or *Human Societies.* Simon and Kahn view growing population as a growing *productive resource* rather than simply, or largely, a growing consumer of resources.

6. *The Coming of Post-Industrial Society,* by Daniel Bell (NY: Basic Books, 1976). One of the few substantial efforts at social forecasting by a sociologist. Although we find the term "postindustrial" inappropriate and misleading (since only the labor force is "postindustrial"), we believe there is much of value here.

7. *Visions: How Science Will Revolutionize the 21st Century,* by Michio Kaku (NY: Doubleday, 1997). A theoretical physicist sees revolutionary developments coming in scientific control of matter, biomolecular engineering, and computers.

8. Books cannot keep up with the rapidity of change in the modern world, and newspapers and magazines are essential. These are five that we have found especially helpful, but there are obviously many more and we encourage you to make use of them: *New York Times, Wall Street Journal, Science News, Science, The Economist,* and *Technology Review.*

QUIZ QUESTIONS

Fill-in-the-Blank

1. The mechanism by which increasing atmospheric pollution is argued to have increased the world's temperature is called the _____ effect.

2. The world's population is currently growing at an annual rate of about ___ percent.

3. Approximately _____ percent of the world's population lives in cities today.

4. At currently projected rates of growth, there will be about ___ billion people in the world by the year 2050.

5. The "higher goals" referred to in Chapter 16 are: (1) _____, (2) _____ , and (3) _____.

6. Patterns of international migration show that people are flowing out of _____ societies, and into _____ societies.

True or False

7. At currently projected rates of population growth, the world will have more than 20 billion people in it by the year 2050.

8. According to Gallup Polls, people in North America are more likely to say they are "very happy" than are people in other parts of the world.

9. The quality of the world's environment would improve significantly if coal were used in place of other fuels and energy sources.

10. In industrial societies, as the freedom of elites increased, the freedom of the average member has declined.

11. We are probably better able to predict future problems than future solutions to problems.

12. Population growth is likely to increase future conflict over access to water.

32. If you were elected secretary-general of the United Nations, what would you target as the most important problems/challenges facing the world in the next century? What would you advocate as solutions to these problems?

Final Exam Essay/Study Questions

1. Which has had the greater impact on human life in the last 150 years: the work of inventors and engineers such as Edison, Bell, the Wright brothers, and Daimler, or the activities of political revolutionaries such as Marx, Engels, Lenin, Stalin, and Mao? Explain.

2. Which has been the more revolutionary force in the modern world, new ideologies or new technologies? In other words, which has had the greater impact on the daily lives of people? Explain.

3. "The study of societal evolution is the study of the great strides humans have made in improving the conditions of life for people. Thanks to technological advance, the conditions of life for most people have steadily improved over the centuries, leading to better health, longer lives, greater freedom, and greater happiness." Do you agree? Explain.

4. The United States and Canada have long enjoyed (a) unusually high standards of living, and (b) unusually democratic systems of government compared to most other societies, past as well as present. Does ecological-evolutionary theory shed any light on the reasons for these unusual features of our societies? Explain.

5. What lessons, if any, can be learned from the massive social experiments conducted by Marxist-Leninist elites in the twentieth century? To what extent are these lessons consistent with ecological-evolutionary theory?

6. René Dubos, a famous biologist, has written, "The past is not dead history, it is living material out of which man shapes the present and builds the future." What evidence can you find from our course to support his claim?

7. If you could choose the type of society into which you were born, *and if modern industrial societies were excluded,* which would you choose, and why? (or, which would you most want to avoid, and why?)

8. "Societal evolution is a problem-creating process every bit as much as it is a problem-solving process." True or false? Explain, drawing on what you have learned this semester.

NOTES

[1] Technically, since even a straight line is a form of curvilinear relationship, the correct terms are *monotonic* and *non-monotonic.* A monotonic relationship is one that consistently moves in one direction (up or down), whereas a non-monotonic relationship *reverses* itself at some point. As we have already seen, trends in fertility, income inequality, and slavery have been non-monotonic with respect to technological advance.

[2] In fact, as we noted in Chapter 13 (pages 280–81), if current total fertility rates continue, many advanced industrial societies will soon be experiencing population *declines*.

[3] If, as was the case in previous technological advances, their populations had grown commensurately, there is every reason to expect that trends in inequality, poverty, and freedom in industrial societies would have continued in their preindustrial pattern. In fact, many of Marx's predictions about increasing misery, polarization, and conflict in industrial societies may well have come true if the "demographic transition" had not occurred.

[4] Some years ago a Chinese official was taking an American on a tour of one of China's industrializing areas. Although the American was greatly concerned and distressed by the coal smoke billowing out of factory smokestacks, the Chinese official was very proud. To him the smoke was not an environmental or health problem; rather, it was a sign of his district's economic progress and development.

[5] It is worth noting that the last major world climate change experienced by humans (global warming about 10,000 years ago) fostered the widespread domestication of plants and animals and spawned what we now term "civilization."

Appendix

Quiz Answers

Introduction

1. hunting and gathering (only 4 percent)
2. agrarian (64 percent)
3. 85 percent (since the percentages add to 100, 100—15 = 85)

Chapter 1

1. (systematic) comparison
2. *macro*sociology
3. signal
4. symbol
5. cooperation ... political autonomy
6. environment
7. ecological-evolutionary
8. genetic and cultural
9. learning
10. adaptation (enhances their chances of survival)
11. biophysical ... social
12. models
13. (biophysical and social) environment ... cultural heritage ... (our species' common) genetic heritage
14. true
15. false
16. false
17. false
18. true
19. true
20. d
21. e
22. d
23. c
24. d
25. d
26. e
27. a
28. b
29. d

Chapter 2

1. system
2. population ... culture ... (material) products of culture ... social organization ... social institutions
3. material product of culture
4. culture (technology)
5. population (demographic variable)
6. social organization (or social institution—stratification)
7. population (demographic variable)
8. population (genetic constant)
9. culture (belief system) or social institution (organized religion)
10. culture (norms)
11. social institution
12. population (genetic variables)

13. (material) product of culture
14. constants ... variables
15. to create and use symbols
16. demographic variables
17. culture
18. socialization
19. ideology
20. capital goods
21. social institutions
22. world system of societies
23. norms
24. stratification
25. true
26. true
27. true
28. false (They are material products of culture.)
29. false (It is a *primary* group.)
30. true

31. false
32. a
33. d
34. b
35. e (It is an aspect of culture.)
36. b
37. a
38. b
39. a
40. b
41. b
42. c
43. a
44. a
45. c
46. c
47. e
48. c

Chapter 3

1. between 8 and 10 million ... 100,000–300,000
2. more than 6.5 *billion* ... less than 200
3. changed dramatically (or advanced) ... didn't change and/or became extinct
4. continuity ... innovation ... selection
5. diffusion
6. alterations
7. discovery ... invention
8. subsistence technology
9. a. the amount of cultural information available to the society
   b. the population size
   c. the stability of the environment
   d. the extent of contact with other societies
   e. the character of the society's biophysical environment
   f. the number of "fundamental" inventions
   g. the society's attitude toward innovation
10. positive
11. evolution
12. sociocultural ... biological

13. false
14. true
15. true
16. false
17. true
18. false
19. false
20. false
21. true
22. true
23. true
24. false
25. d
26. a
27. d
28. e
29. b
30. c
31. d
32. b
33. d
34. e
35. c
36. c
37. a
38. c
39. d
40. d

Chapter 4

1. hybrid
2. subsistence technology
3. environmentally specialized
4. metallurgy
5. subsistence technology ... environment
6. advanced agrarian
7. advanced agrarian
8. hunting and gathering
9. simple horticultural
10. simple horticultural
11. advanced horticultural
12. hunting and gathering
13. industrial
14. agrarian
15. false
16. false
17. false
18. true
19. true
20. false
21. false
22. false
23. true
24. true
25. false
26. true
27. true
28. true
29. e
30. c
31. d
32. a
33. e
34. e
35. c
36. a
37. d
38. e
39. a
40. e

Chapter 5

1. hominids
2. 5 to 6 million
3. 100,000 years ago (when genetically modern humans emerged)
4. 400–600 (or in general terms, a few hundred)
5. 8,500,000 (or between 8 and 10 million)
6. kinship
7. animism
8. shaman or medicine man
9. 50 percent; this indicates that it *supplements* its food with plant cultivation or animal husbandry
10. tribe
11. false
12. true
13. false
14. true
15. true
16. false
17. false
18. true
19. false
20. false
21. false
22. false
23. true
24. true
25. false
26. true
27. d
28. a
29. b
30. e
31. b
32. b
33. d
34. d
35. e
36. e
37. d
38. a
39. b

Chapter 6

1. 10,000–12,000 (8000–10,000 B.C.) ... Middle East (Asia Minor or Southwest Asia)
2. population growth ... environmental change (global warming) ... growth in technological information
3. slash-and-burn ... swidden
4. a forest
5. stop cultivating the land and allow the trees to grow back
6. 4000 B.C. (or 6,000 years ago)
7. copper
8. copper ... tin
9. matrilineal
10. ancestor worship
11. increased incidence of warfare ... ceremonial cannibalism ... human sacrifice ... female infanticide ... head-hunting ... slavery ... high rates of homicide ... patriarchy
12. economic surplus
13. 80 (83 percent to be precise)
14. biology or the genetic heritage of populations (i.e., genetic variables)
15. true
16. true
17. false
18. true
19. false
20. false (the different sequences of development suggest a *multi*linear theory)
21. true (see Table 4.2)
22. false
23. true
24. true
25. true
26. false
27. true
28. a
29. b
30. b
31. c
32. d
33. e
34. c
35. d
36. a
37. e
38. a
39. d
40. d

Chapter 7

1. 3000 B.C. (or about 5,000 years ago) ... Middle East
2. (maintaining) soil fertility ... (fighting) weeds
3. theocracy
4. command
5. between 5 and 10
6. proprietary theory of the state
7. Buddhism ... Christianity ... Islam
8. social environments
9. frontier
10. 15 (Aztec Empire a more conservative estimate is five to six) ... 400 (nineteenth century China)
11. true
12. false
13. true
14. false
15. false
16. true
17. true
18. true
19. false
20. false
21. d
22. e
23. a
24. e
25. d
26. d
27. a
28. d
29. b
30. b
31. a
32. a

33. d	39. c
34. d	40. a
35. d	41. d
36. a	42. a
37. b	43. e
38. c	44. c

Chapter 8

1. fishing	11. b
2. maritime	12. c
3. herding	13. c
4. 700 to 900 (or nearly a billion)	14. b
5. true	15. e
6. true	16. a
7. true	17. b
8. true	18. b
9. false	19. d
10. false	20. a

Chapter 9

1. positive
2. 1760 (mid-eighteenth Century) ... Great Britain (England)
3. growing stores of information ... changing attitudes toward innovation ... the rise of modern science ... the threat of war ... environmental feedback ... the desire for higher standards of living
4. *per capita* Gross National Product (or *per capita* Gross Domestic Product)
5. temperate
6. factory system
7. first
8. third
9. first
10. third
11. first
12. second
13. third
14. fourth

15. false
16. true
17. false (it hasn't ended)
18. false
19. true
20. false
21. true
22. false
23. false
24. false
25. true
26. e
27. c
28. e
29. e
30. e
31. b
32. e
33. e
34. e
35. a

Chapter 10

1. 83–99
2. 13
3. labor ... capital
4. primary (extractive) ... secondary (manufacturing) ... tertiary (services)

5. primary ... tertiary
6. command ... market
7. laissez-faire (or free-market) capitalism
8. 4 ... 50
9. limited
10. false
11. false
12. true
13. false
14. false
15. false
16. true
17. true
18. true
19. false
20. false
21. true
22. true
23. true
24. d
25. c
26. c
27. b
28. b
29. e
30. b
31. a
32. e
33. c

Chapter 11

1. theistic religions
2. secular
3. democratic
4. Adam Smith
5. democratic
6. Karl Marx
7. nationalism
8. pragmatism
9. subjects ... citizens
10. special interest
11. oligarchical ... democratic
12. percentage
13. Protestant Reformation
14. false
15. false
16. false
17. false
18. false
19. true
20. false
21. true
22. true
23. a
24. a
25. d
26. d
27. b
28. a
29. d
30. e
31. a
32. e
33. c
34. a
35. d
36. e
37. d

Chapter 12

1. positive-sum
2. complex
3. 20
4. ascribed
5. 63
6. United States ... Canada ... Denmark
7. false
8. false
9. false
10. false
11. false
12. true
13. true
14. false
15. false
16. false
17. false
18. true
19. true

20. true
21. false
22. false
23. e
24. a
25. e
26. a
27. a
28. e
29. b

30. e
31. b
32. a
33. e
34. a
35. a
36. b
37. c
38. c
39. e

Chapter 13

1. nuclear ... extended
2. the demographic transition
3. communicable diseases
4. 99
5. 20–25 ... 70
6. 2.11 (or a little more than 2)
7. 1.7
8. siblings
9. youth culture (or subculture)
10. 59
11. mass media
12. technological change
13. bachelor's degrees
14. 10 ... (the great majority) 75–90
15. 96
16. true
17. true
18. true
19. false
20. true
21. more than 20

22. true
23. false
24. true
25. true
26. false
27. false
28. false
29. b
30. e
31. e
32. c
33. c
34. b
35. d
36. c
37. a
38. d
39. c
40. d
41. e
42. e

Chapter 14

1. traditional (premodern) subsistence technology, or techno-economic heritage (TEH)
2. See footnote to page 302 of *Human Societies.*
3. See footnote to page 302 of *Human Societies.*
4. industrialization ... modernization or modernity
5. (sub-Saharan) Africa
6. 2.1
7. 2.6
8. China ... India

9. industrializing agrarian
10. 90
11. industrializing horticultural ... industrializing agrarian ... industrial
12. industrializing horticultural ... industrializing agrarian ... industrial
13. industrializing horticultural ... industrializing agrarian ... industrial
14. industrial ... industrializing horticultural/industrializing agrarian (IA and IH societies are virtually tied)
15. industrializing horticultural ... industrializing agrarian ... industrial

16. true
17. false
18. false
19. true
20. true
21. false
22. true
23. true
24. false
25. false
26. true
27. c
28. c

29. b
30. c
31. a
32. a
33. a
34. a
35. c
36. e
37. d
38. d
39. b
40. a
41. d

Chapter 15

1. greenhouse (or global warming)
2. 1.1
3. 50
4. 9.2
5. freedom ... justice ... happiness
6. industrializing ... industrial
7. false
8. true
9. false
10. false
11. true
12. true
13. true

14. false (it's about 15 times larger)
15. true
16. false
17. true
18. c
19. a
20. a
21. d
22. e
23. b
24. a
25. c